SUZANNE FALKINER is a Sydney writer. The author of twelve previous books of fiction and non-fiction, her most recent titles include the biographies *Joan in India*, 2008, and *The Imago: E. L. Grant Watson & Australia*, 2011. She has been shortlisted in the Vogel Award, the Kibble Award, the Queensland Premier's Literary Award, and the NSW History Awards.
www.suzannefalkiner.com

By the same author

Fiction
Rain In The Distance (1986)
After The Great Novelist And Other Stories (1989)

Non-fiction and biography
The Writer's Landscape: Wilderness & Settlement (1992)
Ethel: A Love Story (1996)
Lizard Island: The Journey Of Mary Watson (2001)
with artist Alan Oldfield
Joan In India (2008)
The Imago: E. L. Grant Watson & Australia (2011)
Mrs Mort's Madness (2014)

EUGENIA
A MAN

Suzanne Falkiner

XOUM PUBLISHING

Sydney

 XOUM

First published in 1988 by Pan Books (Australia) Pty Ltd
This edition published by Xoum in 2014

Xoum Publishing
PO Box Q324, QVB Post Office,
NSW 1230, Australia
www.xoum.com.au

ISBN 978-1-922057-79-2 (digital)
ISBN 978-1-922057-80-8 (print)

All rights reserved. Without limiting the rights under copyright below, no part of this publication shall be reproduced, stored in or introduced into a retrieval system, or transmitted in any form or by any means (electronic, mechanical, photocopying, recording or otherwise), without the prior permission of both the copyright holder and the publisher.

Text copyright © Suzanne Falkiner 1988, 2014

The moral right of the author has been asserted.

Cover and internal design and typesetting copyright © Xoum Publishing 2014
Cover photos courtesy NSW Police Forensic Photography Archive, Justice and Police Museum, Historic Houses Trust of NSW and the State Reformatory for Women. Photo description books. State Records New South Wales, by permission of the Department of Corrective Services

Cataloguing-in-publication data is available from the
National Library of Australia

Word count 66,000

Woodrow asked how so, but the whiskey was at work and I felt too deaf to tell him; but what I would have said was: as truth is nonexistent, it can never be anything but illusion—but illusion, the by-product of revealing artifice, can reach the summits nearer the unobtainable peak of Perfect Truth. For example, female impersonators. The impersonator is in fact a man (truth), until he re-creates himself as a woman (illusion)—and of the two, the illusion is the truer.

—Truman Capote, *Answered Prayers*, 1986

Prologue

NEAR MOWBRAY ROAD the Lane Cove River flows smooth and olive green in a rugged chasm carved deep in a bed of sandstone. Among the giant trunks of the surrounding eucalyptus forest a liquid warble of magpies sounds above the song of currawongs and other smaller birds. Below, massive lichened rocks are densely overgrown with ferns and shrubs. The floor of the forest is lightly carpeted with strips of shredded bark and fallen leaves. There is plenty of dead wood lying around, and delicate wildflowers grow here and there among the rocks.

On an early spring morning in 1917, Ernest Clifford Howard, an engineer's apprentice from the nearby Cumberland Paper Mills, was on his way to the mill manager's house when, beside the track, he noticed traces of a scrub fire. He left the path and, in a burnt-out patch of bush, discovered a charred human body. Scattered around were a mundane assortment of objects including a hatpin, the wire framework of a wide-brimmed hat, a table knife, an empty whisky flagon, an enamel mug and a drinking glass, and the remains of a cheap cardboard suitcase. On and near the body were some remnants of inexpensive jewellery.

The boy had taken the same path three days before and noticed nothing unusual. Now this piece of human refuse lay some little distance off the track in a manner that must have appeared horrifying. Parallel to the river, and face upwards, the blackened figure was contorted as if burnt alive. The right leg was sharply drawn up, the arms bent protectively over the chest, the fists clenched. The left side of the chest was so severely burnt that the heart and lungs were exposed. The torso and arms were badly charred and unrecognisable, but the shoes and the lower part of a pair of black stockings were undamaged, as was a strip of gabardine cloth below the buttocks.

To the north, and on the right side of the body, the vegetation was burnt away in a wide circle. To the south, and to the left, the direction from which a fresh southerly wind might have come in the late afternoon of a fine day, there was little burning.

On that morning there might also have been a smell of scorched eucalyptus leaves from a small tree completely destroyed, and a larger one on which the leaves had been seared up to seven metres from the ground. A whirr of grasshoppers might have broken the stillness. The area was sparsely populated, but by no means desolate. A little further on from the paper mills, and over the river, were the Chicago Flour Mills. It was 10.30 a.m. on Tuesday 2 October. On returning to the Cumberland Mills, Ernest Howard telephoned the police.

THE INVESTIGATING POLICE found little that was suspicious. One witness at the subsequent inquiry testified that he had on several occasions seen a woman in a wide hat, carrying a suitcase, in the area. He had thought she might be mentally disturbed. A young female clerk from the Cumberland Mills, at home on her verandah in the late afternoon the day before, had seen smoke and flames coming from the direction of the river. There was no appearance of an attempt to burn the body deliberately, the police concluded. Although there were the remains of a picnic fire or campfire near the body, no fuel had been gathered, no funeral pyre arranged.

After an autopsy had been performed, medical experts gave evidence at an inquest, held before the Acting City Coroner on 31 October of the same year, that the incineration had probably occurred while the woman was still alive and shortly after she had eaten a meal. The empty whisky bottle lent weight to the idea of an accidental death; of a solitary alcoholic who had inadvertently set fire to herself while drunk. The body was thought to be two days old when found, although it was later hypothesised that the fire might have inhibited the appearance of maggots, by the size of which the time of death was estimated. But because the evidence before him did not precisely indicate how death had come about, the coroner gave an open finding. The woman had died of burns caused by her clothing catching fire, he stated, but whether accidentally or otherwise he could not say.

The police officers, Sergeant Maze and Constable Walsh of Chatswood, did not forget the matter of the unidentified woman, however. Three years later, a reopening of the investigation led them to arrest an Italian woman, Eugenia Falleni, who was charged with her murder.

PART ONE

One

ON A COOL AUGUST DAY in 1985, while working as a freelance writer and editor, I found myself on the steps of a convent in Kings Cross, Sydney. By chance, I was to interview one of the nuns for a routine research job, and stood wondering which to press of some confusingly labelled bells. I knew nothing about nuns. The outfit I wore I had consciously chosen as serious and neutral: a black woollen skirt, a grey sweater; and in my leather shoulder bag I had a small tape recorder and a pad with a list of scribbled questions about the early history of one of Sydney's great Catholic hospitals. I felt unexpectedly nervous about what I might encounter. I rang at random one of the bells.

The receiving room of the convent was furnished with some old, polished wood cabinets, a variety of formally arranged antique chairs, some baroque glass and a picture of the Pope. I had never been in a convent before. I had an impression of dark wood and draped curtains, a certain airlessness and stillness of little-used rooms. I talked with the sister who was the convent historian, we shuffled papers on the surface of a polished table, and then I was guided through a labyrinth of passages.

I had expected to meet some form of religious propaganda, but the cheerful Irishwoman who gave me tea in a good porcelain cup, and two slices of homemade cake, and who kissed me on the cheek when I left, rather undermined my melodramatic presuppositions.

In the courtyard we passed through on the way to the archives, I noticed a motley assembly of the nuns' pot plants in highly informal containers, some of which were plastic ice cream cartons. Having impressed me with the good silver and the antique furniture, the historian cast this collection a worried look as she hurried me past.

Their hospital, once a gracious house where in the last century young Irish religious women in flowing veils had fulfilled their vows to serve the sick poor, had become a multimillion-dollar organisation. Some of their number, still wearing an abbreviated version of the veil, were already at home behind computer terminals.

In the early part of this century, I discovered, the hospital had on its staff an Irish doctor, Herbert Michael—'Paddy'—Moran. This man had written a book of memoirs containing an affectionate portrait of the hospital's founders and mainstays, which the historian told me I should read. I had already talked to a retired surgeon, an old raconteur in his Macquarie Street rooms, and he too had mentioned the memoir. It was regarded as quite scandalous at the time, he remarked. Dr Moran had not failed to point out the unsanitary practices and lack of medical expertise of some of the nuns that ran the hospital. The book had caused a sensation on its publication. A wealthy society woman of Irish descent, active in charitable causes, had attempted to buy up the entire edition to protect the reputation of her beloved Mother General.

The sister who was the convent's historian smiled slightly. She had read it herself, she told me. Twice.

When I walked back to my car through the familiar late afternoon streets of Kings Cross, where the seedy sex shows and fast food shops looked a little dispirited in the bright daylight, I felt somewhat curious about this unexplored world of the nuns. Tucked away in the shaded back streets of what had once been a semi-genteel, semi-Bohemian area, many of them continued an antiquated existence of religious ritual behind high walls, and the junkies, voyeurs and tourists in the surrounding streets were barely aware they were there. I had a sense of having ventured into exotic territory.

When I found the memoir, with its stiffened pages and faded cloth covers, H. M. Moran revealed himself as an acerbic middle-aged surgeon with an inquiring mind and some of the prejudices of his generation. His book, *Viewless Winds*,[1] published in 1939, was a mixture of personal experience and medical case studies that had interested him, all interspersed with his own sometimes eccentric opinions, judgements and philosophies. A curious and intelligent sympathy was still fresh in its setting of sometimes mannered prose.

Among his recollections was a brief outline of the story of Eugenia Falleni.

---

1   H. M. Moran, *Viewless Winds*, Peter Davies, London, 1939.

Two

EUGENIA FALLENI, according to Dr Moran, was born in Italy in 1875. In 1877 her family migrated to New Zealand. Moran offered no explanation for this. After traversing half the world to reach a small, isolated, cold island in the Pacific inhabited by Anglo-Saxon sheep farmers and a race of warrior Maoris, they settled in Newtown, a suburb of Wellington in the south of the North Island. But whatever had led them there, they made a go of it. Later police reports stated that the family were law-abiding and held in high esteem.

Eugenia seems to have been the odd note in the success story. Two years old when the family made the long sea voyage, she grew up restless, wilful and undisciplined. She wore boys' clothes when she could and repeatedly ran away from home. On one occasion on 16 September 1891, when 'Nina'—as her family called her—was fifteen, her parents were forced to put an advertisement in the *Wellington Evening Post* asking for information as to her whereabouts. Dressed as a boy, on one occasion she got a job in a brickyard, at another time in a laundry. Small, wiry, strong, dark, unable or unwilling to stay at school or learn to read and write, she was considered 'simple', but her tomboyish eccentricities were regarded as harmless. In her teens, and again dressed as a boy, she ran away to sea.

Eugenia's family did not hear from her again until some years later when she turned up in Newcastle, a seaport on the north coast of New South Wales, having apparently worked in the intervening time as a cabin boy. In her arms was a baby girl, born, again according to Moran, at sea—although a birth certificate from the NSW Registry of Births, Deaths and Marriages indicates that Josephine Falleni was born to 'Lena' Falleni in Double Bay, a suburb of Sydney, on 19 September 1898. The father's surname was not given, and Eugenia's birthplace was entered as 'Leghorn' (or Livorno) in Italy. Her stated age was 23. Moran recounted that Eugenia had been 'violently used' by the captain of the ship and, once pregnant, discarded when the ship docked in New South Wales.

Whatever the facts, Eugenia gave the baby to be fostered by Mariana and Ludovico De Angelis,[2] the Italian couple in whose house in Pelham Street at Double Bay she had borne it, and from then on, for nearly twenty years, she continued to live as a man. It was this same Eugenia Falleni, wrote Moran, who some years later was accused of the murder of the dead woman found near the Lane Cove River.

---

2   Usually given as 'De Anglis'.

Three

I WAS AT SOMETHING of a loose end at the time I came across Moran's version of Eugenia's story. The job I was doing was nearly finished; I had nothing lined up to do next. The house was tidy and the cat stared at me as I sat at the table reading the *Sydney Morning Herald* for too long in the morning. The royalty cheque for the last book I had worked on came in. It was enough to buy me and the photographer lunch. I should have been looking for more work, I knew. But Eugenia niggled at a corner of my mind.

Even before I began to piece it all together, often from contradictory sources, I found my thoughts returning to her against my will. I felt there was something wrong with the story. As I typed up my notes on the Catholic hospital and polished the final piece, I tried to work out what it was. Beyond their obvious oddity, there seemed no internal logic to the events as they were described. The explanation for Eugenia's actions given by Moran, and by the court that convicted her of murder, did not add up. And Eugenia, it appeared, had nowhere offered any explanation herself. Always she was somehow absent from the account. Illiterate, she had written nothing; alone, she had confided in no one.

In addition, how had she survived for as long as she had? It seemed impossible. The society of her time and place denied the existence of those whose gender did not match their sex, allowing, with few exceptions, only for a conventional male or female role. In an Australian working-class milieu—Eugenia was no vaudeville actor or George Sand in a world of posturing bluestockings—her deception had of necessity to be complete. Her life was surrounded by pitfalls. The only question was which might eventually entrap her, despite any amount of vigilance and attention to detail.

Yet, somehow, the impression conveyed—although it was hard to pinpoint on what in Moran's account it was based—was that Eugenia had never thought much about what she was. Her existence was a given; at no time the result of a conscious decision, but a state in which she was born. Like the birds in the garden outside my study, unaware of their birdness.

Some time later I went back to the State Library of New South Wales, where I had found Moran's memoir. I parked my car by the Art Gallery, and carried my folder and pens across the sunlit grass of the Domain. Behind me the shiny glass of the gallery's modern extension leaned solidly against the mellowed stone of the original building, constructed in 1835 by an earnest group of purveyors of false history who called themselves the New South Wales Academy of Art. I could see in my mind's eye the familiar, misleading paintings within: the plump, white-fleshed women with English eyes; the romantic landscapes of harmless golden sunlight and eucalypts beneath hazy skies.

The State Library, built of the same yellow-brown stone, balanced ponderously at the other end of the green lawn, which was punctuated with seagulls. Inside the brass-handled doors, and across the echoing inlaid floors leading to the main gallery, elderly women in cardigans scribbled notes from bound volumes for who knew what arcane projects, safe in the pages of the past. I waited in insulated silence for the newspapers to be brought by an assistant from the stacks. Outside, unheard, cars tore past the brash glass towers on Macquarie Street towards Circular Quay, where Eugenia might have arrived on just such a sunny day, some 86 years before.

IN THE NEWSPAPER section of the library, the yellowing pages of the Sydney dailies revealed that, in the early spring of 1917, the press was mostly concerned with the progress of the First World War. On Wednesday 3 October the front page of the *Evening News* reported that in England the Germans were taking advantage of bright moonlight nights to press air raids on London and the south-eastern counties; while on the European front, despite violent attacks, the enemy was gaining little. The Russians were advancing in the Riga region.

On page four, among the *News*'s usual accounts of the more sensational deaths, divorces and scandals, was a short item headed:

WAS IT MURDER?
Chatswood Mystery Baffles Police
What was Found in the Ashes

The paper explained that although there was insufficient evidence to say whether the woman whose charred body had been found the previous day at Chatswood had been murdered or had burned by accident, several circumstances indicated that another person might have accompanied her to the scene of the tragedy.

The only access to the place where the death occurred was a bridle path used by employees of the paper mills. The woman, who had apparently been lying beside a large rock when the fire took place, was described as being slightly built, and between thirty and forty.

In summary, the reporter detailed the scrap of fawn gabardine found under her body; the common black lace stockings she was wearing, and her half-soled shoes with small homemade patches on the edge of the soles. There was a small piece of floral voile still attached to the wire hat frame found nearby. The fire had apparently started near the woman's chest. Considered significant among the articles found near the body were two drinking vessels: a tumbler and an enamel mug. The police had also found a small piece of bread, and noted that the suitcase was made of compressed paper.

No report had been made of a woman missing.

The *Sun* of Wednesday 3 October, a family newspaper, announced in an almost identical story that, even after a post-mortem examination made by Drs Palmer and Stratford Sheldon, the police were still unsure as to whether they were investigating a murder mystery or an accidental burning. The woman in question was described as thinly built and in poor condition, with brown hair, a piece of which had been found in the ashes.

At 4 p.m. on Monday afternoon employees of the mill had noticed a small fire, but assumed it was lit by picnickers, despite that the spot was unattractive and inaccessible. The body was said to be some 20 yards off the bridle track used by mill employees, and 200 yards off Mowbray Road.

The drinking vessels suggested the presence of more than one person. The stomach contained food, some of which was apparently chicken, and the woman was estimated to have been dead two or three days. There was no evidence of disease or alcohol in the woman's organs. The *Sun* also detailed the broken whisky bottle among the other items found at the site.

On 4 October the *Sun* reported that the body still had not been identified. Police officers had gone over the ashes again and discovered, in addition, a small kidney-shaped greenstone pendant with a short piece of fine chain attached, a number of false teeth from a lower set, two metal buttons and, about six yards away from where the fire had been burning, a bottle in which there was about a spoonful of kerosene.

A number of residents of the district who had female relatives missing had viewed the body, reported the newspaper, but in every instance the dead woman was not the person they sought.

Twelve days later, on Tuesday 16 October, the *Evening News* published a picture of the patched and much-nailed soles of a pair of women's shoes under the heading:

CHATSWOOD MYSTERY
Woman Not Yet Identified
Who patched the Shoes?

Underneath, the paper stated that the investigating detectives had arrived at a dead end. The woman's identity had not been established, and the police wanted to hear from whoever had repaired the shoes.

For about ten days before the death, the report continued, a person thought to be the deceased had been seen about the Chatswood district. This woman was described as about 35, five feet six inches, well-built, wearing a greyish fawn-coloured skirt, white blouse and a large picture hat. She had carried a Japanese wicker suitcase.

As no further developments were immediately forthcoming, the newspapers dropped the story.

Four

OF EUGENIA'S FIRST YEARS in Sydney, much was left unreported in Moran's twenty-page account of her life. Probably she came down from Newcastle by coastal steamer, although the railway line had been completed about ten years before. One can speculate that the slight girl made her way alone from the docks or Central Station—perhaps still dressed in male clothing, despite her pregnancy, and keeping to the identity of a deckhand or a cabin boy—but harbouring the terrifying knowledge of her undoing. Although inhabited by less than a quarter of a million people, Sydney must have seemed daunting after the provincial city of Wellington.

Photographs from the time show steam ferries plying the waters of Sydney Cove and the Parramatta and Lane Cove rivers, tying up at Circular Quay alongside tall-masted ships. The wharves were backed by brick and stone buildings and warehouses of no more than six storeys. From there, the racket of the fishmarkets and the crowded slums of The Rocks gave way to the central business district and the retail area, where the streets were dominated by the big family shopping emporiums. The Town Hall clock, one of the highest structures on the skyline, overlooked streets traversed by horse-drawn cabs, drays and buggies. In the centre of the main thoroughfares, newly electrified trams clanged and dinged over their jointed tracks, with extra passengers standing on the running boards. The streets were crowded with men riding to work on bicycles and boys pushing barrows. The working garb of the day for a man was in hues of heavy brown and grey, with a cheap cotton shirt, the sleeves rolled up, thick-soled work boots and a cloth cap.

Beyond the city centre, with its newly completed monuments to public architecture, working-class suburbs fanned out haphazardly. Sprawls of low, weatherboard and corrugated iron houses with brick chimney pieces, their backyards jammed with outside laundries and water closets and clotheslines, were crammed in beside rows of brick and plaster Victorian terraces. Beyond its industrial fringes, the city petered out into market gardens and farms, and beyond that again were the mountains and the endless plains of the interior. The well-off built their gracious, new English-style mansions on bushy estates in the hills above the sea in the eastern suburbs and to the north, and left the broiling lower areas, considered unhealthy, to the rest. It was a dirty city. In 1900, two years after Eugenia's arrival, there would be an outbreak of bubonic plague, probably due to inadequate drainage and sewerage. Areas like The Rocks, Balmain and the 'North Shore' of the Parramatta River had evil reputations.

Eugenia found herself in a city where bottle-ohs and ice-men with horses and carts made their rounds along with Chinese market gardeners selling door to door.

Shops had tin awnings supported by wooden pillars and upper verandahs decorated with wrought iron lace, and aproned shopkeepers swept the dung from the streets off their shop floors and back out over the footpaths with straw brooms. There was a yellow-tiled pub on every corner, crowded and rough, and open till late at night. In reaction, the temperance movement was strong. In the city centre, the gentry in lace and boaters gathered in Hyde Park on Sundays to listen to the military bands. In three years time, 1901, with much pomp and ceremony and declarations of loyalty to the British Empire, the city elders would celebrate Federation.

From the King Street Wharf in the city a tram ran through Rushcutters Bay to Ocean Street, Edgecliff, on the eastern outskirts. Just below its terminus was the little village of Double Bay. It seems likely that the elderly Italian couple who lived there were known to Eugenia's family in New Zealand. And so it was to Mrs De Angelis's house at 131 Pelham Street—now demolished, but probably a small brick cottage in a row of others, not far from the sea—that Eugenia made her way for shelter.

The basic wage for unskilled workers in the inner city industrial areas was around seven shillings a day or 42 shillings a week for a 48- to 56-hour week. The average wage for women was half that. The age of consent for females in New South Wales was fourteen, and not until 1902, after Federation, would they receive the right to vote. According to a photograph taken some time after this, Eugenia was a slim youth with pale skin, close-cropped hair, large, sensitive eyes and a slightly melancholic mouth.

Shortly after the birth of her baby, wrote Moran, Eugenia, calling herself Harry Crawford and wearing men's clothes, left Double Bay and took a series of menial jobs, usually as a factory hand or general 'useful' at city hotels.

NOW THE DETAILS became patchy. Harry Crawford stayed at nothing for long, Moran reported. For over a decade the young man meandered restlessly all over Sydney and its outskirts, living in boarding houses and on the premises of the pubs where he worked. In a later statement to police, which was marked by certain inventions and omissions, Crawford claimed to have worked initially for six months as a 'useful' at the King's Head Hotel, on the corner of Elizabeth and Park Streets, Sydney. From there he went to a hotel opposite the police station at Temora, where he stayed only a fortnight. He returned to Sydney and was employed at a boarding house near St Patrick's Church, Church Hill, for about three months. Other jobs of a similar nature followed, largely in the inner city. For a time he laboured in the meatworks.

Other sources reveal that occasionally during this decade Crawford visited the house in Double Bay and handed over some of his wages to the Italian woman. By 1910, at the age of twelve, Josephine was earning her own living. Ludovico De Angelis, jealous of his wife's affection for the adopted girl and angered by her refusal to give her up, returned to Italy alone, and both Josephine and Mariana De Angelis were forced to go out and get domestic jobs.

By 1910, too, Harry Crawford's direction had

changed. He found work in the respectable household of Dr Gother Robert Carlyle Clarke, a bachelor in his mid-thirties, at Wahroonga. In his position as a kitchen man and general useful, Harry lived above the stable and chopped wood and drove the doctor's sulky while he made his rounds. Twenty kilometres from Sydney on the northern railway line, Wahroonga, a scattering of gracious houses with large gardens and orchards linked by red clay roads and interspersed with eucalyptus forest, was then a settlement of less than 200 people.

Dr Clarke's house, 'Terranora', was one of two on a large block of land between Coonanbarra Road and Neringbah Avenue on the Lane Cove Road (now part of the Pacific Highway) just opposite a select Church of England school for young ladies. Close by were the railway station and a little cluster of shops.

At Terranora, Harry Crawford met the doctor's general domestic, or cook/housemaid, Annie Birkett. Annie was a 32-year-old widow with one son, also called Harry, then about ten years old. A neat, apparently pleasant-natured woman, she had been at Dr Clarke's for three years. Sometimes Crawford would take the two of them for a drive in the sulky, and he and Annie were often together. He seemed to be courting the widow, bringing her flowers from the garden, taking her on an outing to see a travelling circus that made a one-night stand at nearby Waitara. When, by some accounts, Annie Birkett rejected his advances, complaining of his heavy drinking and improvident ways, he swore he would reform. He reminded her that a growing boy like Harry needed a father's guidance and companionship.

Eugenia: A Man

Three years later, in 1913, Annie Birkett had saved enough money to start up a business of her own. She found a confectionery and soft drink shop in a row of little Victorian, corrugated-iron canopied commercial premises in Darling Street, the main thoroughfare of Balmain, and bought it for £75. Opposite the sedate flower beds, pigeon-covered lawns and palm trees of Gladstone Park, and next to St Andrew's Church, Annie's new home above the shop was in a quite respectable part of the crowded industrial suburb, with its narrow streets of workmen's cottages and foul-smelling factories. According to a statement made later by Annie's son Harry Birkett, Harry Crawford also left Dr Clarke's and followed her.

Crawford took lodgings in Darling Street a little further down the hill from the shop, and frequently visited. He made it appear to the other residents of the street that he was helping Annie with the business. When the neighbours gossiped, Annie apparently felt compelled to accept Crawford's proposal of marriage. About six weeks later, an unsuspecting Methodist clergyman, Mr Hynes, married Harry and Annie at his parsonage in Balmain. Mrs Hynes and Annie's sister Lily Nugent witnessed the ceremony, and Harry gave his father's name as Harry Leo Crawford and his mother's as Louisa Buti.

By this time Harry Crawford was in his late thirties, although he looked a little older. His skin was more weathered than one might expect in a man of his age. He had thickened somewhat, and appeared, at five foot four inches (or 163 cm), a short, stocky man, but not heavily built, with grey eyes and a beardless face. His hair was dark brown, short, brushed straight back, and usually hidden under his grey felt hat. His hands were broad and blunt. He customarily dressed in the ordinary grey trousers and jacket—long enough to cover his buttocks—worn by most working men of the period. He walked with short, quick, nervous steps, swinging his arms from the shoulders.

To a casual observer his dark hair and his colouring might have suggested Gaelic origins, but his English was rough, often profane, with some of the incorrect tenses often associated with a foreigner. However, there was something about him that seems to have made women lower their guard to him—the middle-aged women battling with domestic drudgery who lived in the working-class suburbs through which he drifted from job to job. He was always willing to talk. Conceivably, to them, he possessed a certain uncharacteristic softness, an understanding, a certain persuasiveness of character, although he was as much a drinker and swearer as most of the other men in the pubs and meat packing factories in which he worked.

Five

SEVEN OR EIGHT MONTHS after his marriage in 1913, wrote Moran, Harry Crawford, who was now working at the National Meatworks, Balmain, began to show signs of discontent. He was drinking heavily and was abusive to his wife, and young Harry Birkett, Annie's son, distrusted him. The sweet shop was not financially successful, and Harry and Annie quarrelled frequently. Finally, the household broke up.

Annie Birkett sold the shop at a severe loss and went to stay for a few weeks with her sister, Lily, taking young Harry with her. Lily and her husband, Hugh Nugent, lived in Kogarah, a semi-rural southern suburb surrounded by market gardens, about eighteen kilometres from the city centre and near the flat waters of Botany Bay. Their house was one of a row of brick bungalows in Robertson Street, on the corner of Queen Victoria Street, not far from the Kogarah railway station.

After a while Annie returned to being a domestic servant, this time for a Dr Binns in nearby Belgrave Street, where she stayed for over a year. But Harry continued to visit her, and made persistent attempts to persuade her to come back to him. Annie, harassed, again left her job. She rented a house in a line of small weatherboard or brick workmen's cottages in Austral Street, Kogarah, and furnished it. While at this cottage, Crawford made up his differences with her and again moved in.

According to young Harry's deposition to police, at this time his behaviour again became objectionable, and during arguments he broke up furniture and pulled up plants in the yard. The household finally settled again in a rented house at No 7 The Avenue, Drummoyne, an inner-city suburb, and Harry got a job at Perdriau's rubber factory, makers of motor car tyres, waterproof clothing and other rubber goods, at Petersham. Soon after, they moved house again to No 5 The Avenue, next door. Young Harry Birkett, after he left the public school at Drummoyne in 1916, worked full-time at the local grocery shop on the corner of Lyons Road and The Avenue, for which in his schooldays he had run messages. He was twelve years old. Annie occasionally went out to do washing and housework.

Around this time, according to Moran, Josephine also came to live with the household. Her foster mother Mariana De Angelis had died intestate on 29 October 1913, and Josephine had stayed for a short time with Annie and Harry at Balmain, before going away to work in a factory. By one account a quietly-spoken but moody girl with long black hair, Josephine was around fifteen at the time of her first visit. Soon after she returned, this time pregnant with an illegitimate child, and Harry took her in again, ostensibly as her father, before finding her lodgings with a Mrs Keith of Hoffman's Lane in Balmain.

Josephine gave birth at St Margaret's Maternity home in Bourke Street, Darlinghurst. She called the baby Josephine De Anglis, but the infant died on 10 December 1914, at three months, of a heart defect.

Who knew what about Harry Crawford at this stage was fairly straightforward. Josephine herself knew that her mother was pretending to be a man. Annie was apparently still in ignorance, and assumed that Harry, her husband, was indeed Josephine's father. According to Moran's account, the neighbours accepted Harry as a man, as Josephine's father and Annie's husband, and treated Josephine kindly.

Some time in January 1917, says Moran, when Josephine was aged nineteen and Harry 42, Josephine, pestered by neighbours' questions as to the whereabouts of her mother, let slip the truth.

'There is my mother over there, dressed up as a man,' she said in exasperation. Moran recounts that it was a very short time before one of the neighbours was unable to resist sharing the secret with Annie.

Other unrelated sources profess that it was not until early September of 1917 that Annie sent a letter to a relative, presumably Lily, about the matter. 'I've found out something queer about Harry,' she wrote. 'I don't know what to do, but I'll tell you about it when I see you and get your advice.' Yet another account has it that she confided the same thing to a neighbour. Although she seems to have said little to anyone, something apparently got back to Harry, and he guessed that she knew.

Now Harry was thrown into turmoil, wrote Moran.

He began to follow his wife incessantly, never letting her out of his presence, allowing her no privacy with anyone else. At some point, while on a visit to her sister with Harry, Annie managed to tell Lily Nugent of her dilemma under cover of a trip to the W. C. Lily advised Annie to demand that Harry disprove the story, and Harry, of course, could not. For the sake of her son, Moran maintains, Annie apparently decided to continue as normal, but to take steps to have the marriage quietly annulled. Yet she did nothing. Eight months later (if Moran's dates are correct) they were still together, with Annie unhappy, Harry increasingly bad-tempered towards her, and still drinking and using violent language.

On 28 September 1917, the Friday before the Labour Day weekend, the couple, apparently quite amicably, were seen to go out together to have a picnic on the Lane Cove River. Annie Birkett was not sighted again.

Six

THE TRAIL from the newspaper files led obviously to the New South Wales Government Archives, which yielded a transcript of Eugenia's trial. After I had corresponded with the Solicitor for Public Prosecutions, the Archives also gave up the deposition that had led to Eugenia's arrest. Blanks were drawn at the Police Department and the Department of Corrective Services. The files no longer existed in most cases, I was told. I made other telephone calls and wrote letters. I waited months for correspondence to be answered in some cases, merely days in others. Usually, I was referred back to the Government Archives. The precise dates of the trial, and the proceedings leading up to it, enabled me to go back to the newspaper files. Then I took on another editing job. Meanwhile, despite maddening gaps in the available information, the details began to build into a picture.

It was not until three years after the charred body had been found at Lane Cove that the police made further progress with the case. This occurred on 13 June 1920 at the Criminal Investigation Branch in Sydney when seventeen-year-old Harry Bell Birkett, a tailor's apprentice residing at 'St George', The Avenue,

Sans Souci, the residence of Frank Bombelli, made a deposition to police. As a result, on the morning of Monday 5 July of the same year, Detective Sergeant Stewart Robson, Constable Walsh and Detective Constable W. C. Watkins went to the Empire Hotel on the corner of Parramatta Road and Johnston Street, Annandale. Here they found Harry Crawford washing beer glasses in the cellar and persuaded him to accompany them to the Central Police Station at Central Street in the Haymarket for questioning.

On the same day Detective Sergeant Robson, in Crawford's presence, searched a house about half a mile away from the hotel, at 47 Durham Street near Stanmore railway station. The narrow-fronted, one-storey cottage with a tiled roof, distinguished from its neighbours by a bay window, stood in a barren street where a few thin eucalyptus trees provided little shelter from the midday sun. In front was a small square yard guarded by a wrought iron fence.

In the room where Harry Crawford had been living with Elizabeth King Allison, the woman he had made his second wife, Robson went methodically through the couple's possessions. Among them was a handsome solid leather suitcase, initialled in gold H. L. C., which was locked. Inside, the detective found a pair of well-tailored trousers in blue cheviot serge; some cufflinks, sleeve suspenders, collars and socks; a partly-loaded revolver; and an object, never fully identified or described in the court transcripts or newspapers, that Robson carefully took away as evidence against the day when Harry would be put on trial.

Eugenia: A Man

BETWEEN HARRY CRAWFORD'S being taken into custody on 5 July and Eugenia Falleni's trial three months later on 5 October, Detectives Robson and Watkins of the Sydney Police worked hard and methodically to construct their case. In the intervening weeks, with other police officers, they interviewed several hundred people and subpoenaed over forty witnesses.

On Tuesday 6 July, when Eugenia first appeared at the Central Police Court before Mr Jennings, SM, the court was crowded with spectators. The *Evening News* of that day, which followed the saga closely over the next month, noted that 'though apparently unconcerned, the accused was very pale'. She was dressed in a dark grey suit of men's clothes, a white turn-down collar, 'Broadway' tie, soft tennis shirt, and patent leather lace-up boots. She carried a soft grey felt hat, and wore a gold ring on a finger of her left hand.

The same paper printed a photograph of Eugenia as she appeared leaving the court after the proceedings. This was a blurred image of an apparently male figure, with mouth set in a grim line and eyes shaded by a hat. Beside it was a studio portrait, head and shoulders, of Annie Birkett. This conveyed an impression of a remarkably pretty woman, probably in her early thirties at the time the photograph was taken, with fine, regular features and luxuriant dark hair piled on top of her head. She wore a high-necked, lace-trimmed blouse in white and what appeared to be pearl stud earrings.

During the proceedings, the paper continued, Sergeant White, police prosecutor, had asked Mr Jennings, the magistrate, to refuse bail. Mr Maddocks

Cohen, who appeared for the defence, stated that he did not intend to ask for bail. Eugenia was remanded to 14 July, eight days later.

The *Evening News* followed these details with a brief but largely fictitious version of Eugenia's life story, no doubt based on what she herself had told police after her arrest. According to this account, Eugenia was Italian, had married in Italy, and had one daughter. On leaving her native country she had gone to New Zealand, where she had lived for some years before coming with her daughter to Sydney. Shortly afterwards she had adopted male attire, and later, under the name 'Harry Crawford', married a widow named Birkett, living at Wahroonga, with whom she had gone to live at Drummoyne.

On the same day the *Sun* printed a six-by-four inch clear photograph of Eugenia, whom the accompanying article described as 'strangely interesting'. The picture was apparently taken as Eugenia stood between two detectives in suits. The paper mentioned the large crowd at the Central Police Court.

Eugenia Falleni as she appeared at the Sydney Central Police Court on the first day of the committal proceedings. 'Though apparently unconcerned, the accused was very pale', commented one newspaper. There was a large crowd of spectators to witness her arrival and departure. Photo: *Sun*, 6 July 1920

Falleni bore an extraordinary resemblance to a man, the reporter from the *Sun* continued. Her short, almost black hair was parted on the left side, her head and face were remarkably small, and the fact that her face was considerably wrinkled around the mouth suggested that she was older than her stated age of 45 years. Her boots, he wrote, were well polished and appeared to be about size six.

On Wednesday 7 July, under the heading 'The Man-Woman', the *Evening News* again took up the story. Mrs Birkett, whose maiden name was Annie Bell, was born in Newcastle in 1876 and married to Harry Birkett at St John's Church, Darlinghurst, in 1904. Her husband had died shortly after her child, a boy, was born. The widow later went into domestic service, and was employed by Judge Curlewis[3] at his home in North Sydney, and later by Dr Clarke at Wahroonga.

Annie Birkett, circa 1910, from a studio portrait similar to one tendered as an exhibit at Eugenia Falleni's trial. Photo: *Evening News*, 6 July 1920

Eugenia's alleged life story was also further elaborated upon. While still living in Italy, the story now went, she had met and married a man called Martello, with whom she had gone to New Zealand. Leaving her husband there, but bringing her daughter Josephine, she had come to Australia. In Australia she had adopted male attire, being known as Eugene Martello, Eugene (or sometimes Gene) Falleni, Harry Crawford, or Harry Leon Crawford. Falleni had worked as a useful at various hotels in the city, and the National

---

3   Judge Herbert Curlewis was the husband of popular children's author Ethel Turner, and the couple lived at 'Avanel', overlooking Middle Harbour.

Meat Company, before going to Dr Clarke's, where she met the woman she was accused of murdering.

On the same day, 7 July, the *Daily Telegraph* published a large, clear photograph captioned: 'Eugene Falleni leaving the Central Police Court with Detective Sergeant Robson, the officer in charge of the case'. Eugenia appeared as a small man in a neat suit and tie, at least half a head shorter than the heavily built, middle-aged detective who walked beside him. The journalist from the *Telegraph* maintained that 'though the woman was facially masculine, a close scrutiny betrayed feminine characteristics'. This rather contradicted the journalist writing for the *Sunday Truth* of 11 July, who had apparently perceived signs of shaving on the prisoner's skin. The *Evening News* added that application had been made to exhume the body of Annie Birkett.

Eugenia Falleni leaving the Central Police Court with Detective Sergeant Stewart Robson, the officer in charge of the case.
Photo: *Daily Telegraph*, 7 July 1920

On Thursday 8 July the *Evening News* breathlessly continued the saga. The police were energetically pursuing their inquiries, and every day new and interesting facts were brought to light, reported the paper. The case was revealing a story of mystery, cunning, and clever investigation.

After Annie Birkett's disappearance, the *News* revealed, Falleni and the boy Harry Birkett had left the house in The Avenue, Drummoyne, and lived in various places around the city. Later Falleni left the boy, who subsequently lived alone and worked at whatever he could get in warehouses and other places.

During this time, continued the paper, Harry Birkett, then about fifteen years of age, did not appear to have given serious thought to his mother's whereabouts. About three years later, however, determined to trace her, he found out that his aunt, Annie's sister, was now living at Kogarah. On going to see her, he was surprised to find that she thought his mother had been with him all the time. It was then that he discovered that none of her relations had heard from her since September 1917.

In May 1920 Harry Birkett and his aunt had reported Annie Birkett as a missing person. Harry suggested that the body found at Lane Cove at the time his mother had disappeared might have been hers. The police, reinvestigating the dead woman's identity, decided to arrest Falleni and charge her with murder.

Last night, reported the *Evening News*, Detective Watkins had visited a dentist, a Mr Vernon, who was believed to have done some dental work for the dead woman in 1909. The police were still trying to trace the burial place of Mrs Birkett, whose unidentified remains had been buried in the unknown paupers' section at Rookwood. The *News* concluded:

> A feature of the case, fascinating in its revelation of the eccentricities of human nature, is the apparently sincere attachment, which exists between Falleni and the woman who now passes as her wife.
>
> This woman has protested passionately to the police that Falleni is her dear and loving husband, and nothing will shake that statement. She protests an affection for Falleni

which is astonishing in its strength, and
would be so even between man and wife.

On 8 July the *Daily Telegraph* had its own developments to reveal. Falleni, it seemed, had lived and worked for some time at Double Bay. Local residents had recognised her at once from the photograph published in the *Telegraph* the day before. Several people, when questioned, admitted that it had been known for some time that Falleni, dressed as a man, was actually a woman.

These informants said that Falleni and her daughter had lived with an elderly Italian woman and her husband in a cottage in Pelham Street in Double Bay, where a laundry business was conducted. Falleni had earlier been seen at work there in women's attire, but the residents later saw her driving a laundry cart while dressed as a man.

The daughter, they said, was known as 'Eenie'—short for Josephine—and was in the habit of addressing her mother as 'mother', even when she was dressed in male clothing. Sometime after the elderly Italian woman had died, Crawford, as Falleni was known, had worked with Josephine in a meat factory at Riverstone. On one occasion Falleni's fingers had been caught in a machine. 'Come quickly, your father has his fingers caught!' an employee had called out to Josephine.

Josephine, recalling the incident afterwards, said to friends that she was afraid her mother would be recognised as a woman at the hospital should she be taken there. Her mother, however, had bandaged her injury herself.

Eugenia: A Man

EUGENIA MADE a second appearance before the bench eight days later. On Wednesday 14 July the court was again crowded with spectators waiting to gawk at the 'man-woman', as the papers continued to call her. However, before Eugenia was due to appear the court was cleared to allow a first offender to be charged and remanded. The reporter from the *Evening News* of that day noted a look of disappointment on the faces of the spectators as they filed out and impatiently waited outside. When the doors were re-opened fifteen minutes later, they rushed in and struggled for positions. Eugenia, still dressed as a man, was now hidden from them by the dock. According to the same paper, she appeared unconcerned.

The *Evening News* accompanied its front page story with a full length photograph of Eugenia entering the court house. This portrayed a stocky man in a slightly baggy suit standing squarely, his hands behind his back. The corners of his mouth drooped downwards. His features were strong, but not unpleasantly so, and the jaw prominent. He looked distressed but not cowering. A grey felt hat was set firmly on his head, and he wore a waistcoat and a tie.

Sergeant White, the police prosecutor, asked for a further remand until 22 July, as the police were still completing their inquiries, he reported. The magistrate, Mr Butler, granted this.

Mr Cohen, for the defence, complained that it would be useless to remand Eugenia until then if the police would still not be ready. He understood there was to be an inquest, he added, and his client did not wish to be paraded before the court in the meantime. He suggested a longer adjournment, till 29 July, and this was granted. Eugenia was then removed from the dock unseen by the crowd.

On 14 July the *Sun* also printed another photo, full length, but not as clear as its previous ones.

Eugenia Falleni... at her second appearance at the committal proceedings, nine days after her arrest. Photo: *Evening News*, 14 July 1920

'If Eugene Falleni, who has been designated the man-woman, were taken into the forum like the Romans were in bygone days,' the accompanying story began, 'probably the whole of the Metropolis would turn out to get a glimpse of her.'

The crowd assembled at the Police Court was described as huge. Falleni kept her right hand under the lapel of her coat, and her expression was worried and anxious, the paper continued.

> Miss Josephine Falleni, the daughter of
> Eugene Falleni, was at Police Headquarters
> this afternoon. She was brought there by
> Detective Sergeant Robson and Detective
> Watkins. A remarkably pretty girl, with very
> dark hair and brown eyes, Miss Falleni made
> some interesting statements to police. She said
> she had been employed at Pyrmont at a jam
> factory for some years and had only seen her
> mother occasionally during the last few years.

Truth of Sunday 18 July supplied more details of Josephine's alleged parentage. The previous version, that a little over 22 years before, Eugenia and her husband Martello had together left Italy for New Zealand, and that Falleni had afterwards come to Sydney alone with her daughter, was apparently discounted. Now it was claimed that Falleni, who had gone from Italy to New Zealand with her parents as a small child, had met Martello, the captain of an Italian ship, in New Zealand, and they had formed an attachment. She had subsequently left her parents to become his wife. After sailing in his vessel with the child of their union, Falleni and the baby were landed in Newcastle. Falleni had then made her way to Sydney and adopted male attire.

Falleni was alleged to have treated her daughter roughly, *Truth* continued. Josephine, having worked in a city warehouse until she heard of the charge against her mother, had then 'lived privately', making it difficult for police to find her. She was said to be an intelligent and well-spoken girl, the paper finished.

Despite Mr Cohen's efforts to keep Eugenia out of

the courts, the *Evening News* of Wednesday 21 July reported that Falleni had once again appeared before Mr Butler, SM, that day, still in male clothing and apparently little interested in the proceedings. A further remand was requested, on the grounds that the police were making inquiries in New Zealand and Newcastle. It was stated that no second inquest would be held. The date for Eugenia's next appearance was reaffirmed as 29 July.

On 22 July the paper disclosed that the previous day the City Coroner, Mr John Jamieson, had ordered that the body of Annie Birkett be exhumed at Rookwood cemetery, and exhaustively re-examined by Drs Palmer and Sheldon at the City Morgue. When the coffin was opened, the *Evening News* reported, it was seen to contain practically nothing but a handful of ashes. However, the police hoped that a cause of death—if a metal bullet or a mineral poison—might still be identified.

In fact, the coffin, opened at the old 'dead house' of convict days at 104 George Street, contained Annie's three-year-old disintegrating skeleton overlaid with a gruesome layer of decomposed tissue. Eugenia, *Truth* of Sunday 25 July revealed, was escorted in to view it immediately after the coffin was opened. If the police had hoped to shock a confession from her by this macabre act, they were disappointed. Eugenia remained silent, and glanced only briefly at the decayed remains.

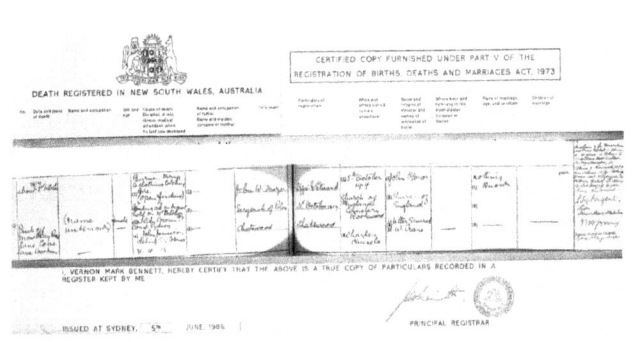

Annie Birkett's death certificate, originally dated 'about 10 October 1917', altered 3 August 1920.
Photo: NSW Registry of Births, Deaths and Marriages

On 29 July Eugenia made her fourth appearance, again a brief one. The *Evening News* that day reported the court was again crowded, mainly with women, who had waited an hour to be let in and who pushed and struggled for places. Again the court was cleared to deal with a first offender. Before the crowd could regain their positions, Eugenia was brought in and, in less than two minutes, was once more remanded. Maddocks Cohen expressed a hope that the police would soon be ready to proceed. The Magistrate, Mr Edwards, told him that the police claimed that this would be the last adjournment.

The *Sun* of 29 July added to this that:

> while the charge was being read, Falleni stood
> erect, gripping the rail of the dock with both
> hands. She was still in male attire, and did
> not appear to heed what was going on in the
> court. She fixed her eyes on the ceiling, and
> only occasionally turned her head, when she
> swept a swift glance over the public quarter
> of the court.

Among the odd bits of intelligence the newspapers revealed during this period was the reason Eugenia had allegedly given police for assuming a male personality. Falleni, *Truth* of Sunday 11 July reported, had said that because, in comparison, women worked long hours for a small wage, she considered she was better off as a man. She regarded herself as quite competent to do the work of a hotel useful, and other forms of manual labour, and did so, working for fewer hours and more money than if she had 'remained' a woman.

Eugenia: A Man

Three police department photographs of inscribed 'Eugene Falleni', probably taken on the day she was charged. Note that she is hiding her right hand, with the missing little finger, as was her habit. Photo: NSW Police Forensic Photography Archive, Justice and Police Museum, Historic Houses Trust of NSW

Suzanne Falkiner

Seven

EUGENIA, I could only conclude, was driven by a strong psychological compulsion to live as a man, despite her apparently normal physiology as a woman. Such a condition was no longer as mysterious as it was. Female transsexuals (and transgenders) had spoken of a conviction that they were born with the mind of a man in the body of a woman, and those of both sexes have undergone surgery to enable them to live more fully the role that matches their gender. Yet if Eugenia were governed in her deceptions by a powerful inner need, her external circumstances might only abet her desire for the transformation.

Eugenia, as an Italian woman, was part of a sexual minority among an ethnic minority from which she had already excluded herself on both counts. In early twentieth century Australia and New Zealand, and particularly in a working-class milieu, there was little enough value in being an Italian or a woman.

From the 1870s onwards, for political and economic reasons, a small but steady flow of Italian migrants to Australia had begun. The migrants were initially male, mainly from the north of Italy, and came without Government assistance. As in New Zealand, they worked as labourers or in family concerns while accumulating money to start their own farms, shops and other businesses, and then, in chains of family migration, they brought out their friends and relatives. Only five or six in every hundred were women. Adventurous people, they were also establishing communities in North and South America as well as in Australia and New Zealand.

By 1920, when Eugenia Falleni was arrested and tried for the murder of Annie Birkett, there were a little over 8000 Italians in Australia, and still under 2000 of them were women. Although scattered all over Australia, they were united by a network of family links, and often existed in single units of tight-knit family groups.

This cohesiveness was not entirely a matter of choice. *The Immigration Act* of 1901, which came in within two years of Eugenia's arrival, restricted the entry of Southern European migrants, and this reflected a current social attitude that Australians should be white and preferably of British origin. Southern Europeans, from their first entry in sizeable numbers in the days of the gold rushes, were considered to have lower living standards, and were not readily accepted into the wider community, or readily employed by Anglo-Saxon Australians.

If Eugenia had improved her chances of employment by adopting an Anglo-Saxon name, she also improved her economic prospects by becoming a man.

Eugenia had arrived in Australia in her early twenties in a society where (according to the 1901 and 1911 Censuses) a little over 82 per cent of all women were described as 'dependants'—housewives and mothers, or as yet unmarried daughters still living with their families. Fewer than 20 per cent were employed, and these mainly in menial positions as factory workers and domestic servants, although some were shop assistants and teachers or governesses. Wages for women were less than half the usual wage for men. Their pay and working conditions were not a concern of the almost completely male industrial unions, except where, as cheap labour, they threatened the jobs of men. They were eligible for few social services beyond widows' pensions and child endowment—legislation that was aimed at supporting the institution of marriage. In all classes, therefore, to aspire to marriage and motherhood was a woman's only practical goal. It was certainly that of Harry Crawford's wives, Annie Birkett and Lizzie Allison. Any other form of existence was eccentric, a sign of failure, or morally questionable. Even widows, more honourable failures in the marriage stakes than divorcees and spinsters, did not have the same social status as married women, or the same legal rights. Eugenia, as a young woman with an illegitimate child, no family in Australia to shelter her, and no real aspirations to wifehood, faced a very limited future.

After 'becoming' a man, Eugenia/Harry Crawford seemed to want the same things in a wife as did most Australian men of the period: including a respectable woman who would make him a home. He wanted a comfortable kitchen where he could relax after work with a beer or a whisky, and to have his meals cooked and his shirts washed. If the woman contributed to his wellbeing with a little cash of her own, so much the better. Harry Crawford, more than anything, it seems, wanted to be an ordinary man, married to an ordinary woman.

WAS IT this suburban ordinariness, then, that drew him to Annie Birkett, widow, domestic servant, daughter of a storekeeper migrated from Durham in England? Or was it that now, tired of wandering, he saw a chance to settle down, and felt the two of them together could make the home they both needed? Annie Laura Bell, according to her birth certificate, and contrary to the report in the *Evening News*, was born in Lambton, Newcastle, New South Wales, on 11 March 1878, to George Edward Bell and Emily Bell, née Woodgate. Emily was herself born in Victoria. Emily and George were both 21 at the time of her birth, and had married on 2 August the year before.

Annie's own son, Harry, was born on 6 January 1903, at 43 Anglesea Street, Bondi, when Annie was 25. She married his father, a 33-year-old English tailor, Harry Birkett, at Darlinghurst, Sydney, two months later on 5 March 1903, and was left a widow just three years after that.

Harry Birkett senior had been born in Nottingham, England, the son of a farmer, William Birkett, and Mary, née Limbert. He had come to New South Wales in 1899, four years before marrying Annie. He died of heart failure at Newcastle hospital on 11 January 1906 after an illness lasting some months, and was buried at the Church of England cemetery at Newcastle. The fact that Annie and Harry were married in Sydney after the birth of her child, while Harry was hospitalised and died in Newcastle, suggests that the couple may not have lived together for all the three years of their marriage, or that it may have been a marriage in name only. Annie's sister, Lily Bell, then living at Barcom Avenue, Darlinghurst, supplied the details for the death certificate.

When Annie's body was finally identified in 1920, it would again be Lily, now Nugent, and now living at Stuart Street, Blakehurst, who would supply the necessary details for the death certificate. And it was Lily who had officially witnessed Annie's and Harry Crawford's marriage.

Annie Birkett was 39 at the time of her death. According to the *Police Gazette* of 25 August 1920, the length of the corpse of the unidentified woman found dead at Chatswood was 'five feet seven inches'. She had false teeth in her upper and lower jaw—not uncommon at a time when it was quite customary to have healthy teeth removed to avoid subsequent dental problems. A complete set of false teeth could be obtained from a dentist for about two pounds ten shillings.

In the opinions of her neighbours, Annie was a quiet, temperate woman, and one who kept her troubles to herself. She wore conservative clothing, had saved money and collected some small articles of jewellery, and she liked quality in her linen and household effects, which she kept scrupulously clean. A respectable woman, she kept a respectable household. Her marriage had been short, but presumably she was not completely sexually inexperienced after conceiving a child. Having been widowed early in her first marriage, she later had tried to become independent in her own small business.

So, Annie Birkett. Was it weakness that allowed

Harry Crawford to wear her down, by some accounts to marry her almost against her will? Was there some habit of submission in her, that he recognised and exploited, that drew her to him?

Annie Birkett met Harry Crawford in 1910, when she was 32. The two were married in Balmain three years later, when Annie was 35 and Harry was 38. They had lived together, on and off, as man and wife for four years. According to all the evidence, most of those years were not happy, and the last year even less so.

Perhaps it was merely inertia, or the fear of being alone again, that stopped Annie Birkett from leaving Harry when she discovered his secret. Perhaps it was fear of scandal, which after all had partly motivated her to marry Harry, that led her to keep up a pretence of normality. Perhaps, having lost her savings, she saw Harry's labourer's wage as keeping her from a return to a life of drudgery as a household servant. Perhaps it was habit. Perhaps she loved him, despite all. Perhaps she intended to leave him, but never did. She made no initial move to have the marriage annulled, as Moran had suggested she intended, but this may have been from ignorance of how to go about it.

Once his secret was discovered, Harry Crawford, for similarly unknowable reasons, did not attempt to leave her.

Eight

WHEN EUGENIA was remanded for the last time, she had been in gaol for nearly a month. She had been put through an exhausting and nerve-wracking procession of court appearances, attended by delays and uncertainty as to what would happen next. Now she was held for another two weeks before appearing in the Central Police Court on 16, 18 and 19 August, at the end of which she was finally committed for trial.

Once again the court was crowded and reporters from a number of Sydney newspapers were present. Much column space was devoted to summarisations of the testimony of witnesses. The *Evening News* devoted three quarters of a page to each of the three days of the proceedings. *Truth* of Sunday 22 August also picked up the story in detail, giving over an entire page to the case, with sketches of all the leading witnesses and of Eugenia herself.

'Eugene' Falleni, alias Eugene Martello, alias Harry Crawford, alias Harry Leon Crawford, 45, described as a 'general useful', was charged with the felonious and malicious murder of Annie Birkett or Crawford, on or about 1 October 1917, according to the charge sheet. The presiding magistrate was Mr C. H. Gale;

Mr Roderick Robert Kidston of the Crown Law Office conducted the case for the prosecution; and Mr Maddocks Cohen, an experienced criminal lawyer assigned by Legal Aid, appeared for the accused.

Just after ten o'clock Eugenia was ushered into the dock, neatly dressed in a well-worn grey suit, blue serge vest and a big blue tie. Her hair, according to the *News*, was 'plastered down in the ordinary masculine fashion' above a white collar. She was thin, pale and haggard, and while the charge was being read, her hands picked nervously at the dock rail. In reply she said, 'Not guilty' in a low voice, and sat down on the dock bench.

Kidston opened the case, remarking to the court that he would refer to the accused as a male person, as all the witnesses knew her as a male.

Rod Kidston—still in his late twenties, but descended from a legal family and known for his detailed knowledge of the law—called a number of witnesses who gave lengthy testimony, most of which was later duplicated at the trial. A few points arose which did not re-emerge as evidence, although the press reported them extensively. Extracts from Josephine and Eugenia Falleni's signed statements to police were also printed almost in their entirety, suggesting that copies were made available to reporters. Lizzie Allison was not called, however: pestered by journalists and curiosity seekers since her neighbourhood address had been revealed, she had evidently since disappeared.

The first witness called by the prosecution was Constable John H. Walsh of North Sydney, who had found the remains of the body near the paper mills on

Eugenia: A Man

2 October 1917. He had first seen the accused on 22 July 1920, at the Central Police Court, he said, when she was placed in a line with a number of men. Falleni, wearing male clothing, had been identified in the line-up by a man named Hicks.

Subsequently he went with Hicks, Falleni, and other police officers to the spot near the mills. After first denying that she had ever been in the area, Falleni admitted working in the flour mills at one time.

Maddocks Cohen tried for his first point in Eugenia's defence. Addressing Walsh, he asked, 'Hicks identified the woman?'

'Yes. As having been at Lane Cove in 1917,' answered the constable.

'The photograph of the accused appeared in all the papers before 22 July, when the identification was made?'

'It had appeared in certain papers,' admitted Walsh. Here Kidston put a query: 'Did Mr Hicks know in connection with what cause he was making the identifications?'

'After the whole world knew about the man-woman!' exclaimed Cohen.

Some time after this exchange, Acting Inspector Maze, who at the time of the death had been a police sergeant at Chatswood, and who had been with Constable Walsh at the finding of the body, admitted to Mr Cohen that he had said at the Coroner's Court that he thought the woman had accidentally or deliberately set fire to herself. He had afterwards stated that he felt it more likely that she had caught fire accidentally, he said. There was no sign of a struggle, no inflammable material round the body, and the fire afterwards seemed to have burnt itself out.

Maze agreed with Cohen that he had received a complaint at the time about a woman who acted in a suspicious manner, entering houses in the area during the day and at night. In answer to Kidston, Maze said that he felt the matter of the wandering woman had been cleared up satisfactorily.

Two dentists, John F. McManus and Dr H. G. Vernon, now identified the false teeth produced in court as consistent with work they had performed for Mrs Birkett. To Cohen, McManus admitted reading of the story in the newspapers before giving evidence, and also that he had supplied a good many patients with sets of false teeth. He said he did not remember the work specifically, but that he remembered the name of the woman distinctly, and he had identified the work from his ledger. He also remembered the small boy who was her son.

Mrs Lily Nugent, of Stewart Street, Blakehurst, who was Annie Birkett's sister, testified to Kidston that she had been present when her sister 'married' the accused. Only the parson, the parson's wife, her sister, herself and Crawford had been at the marriage ceremony, which had taken place at the parsonage in Balmain.

Lily Nugent identified a heart-shaped greenstone pendant and chain, and a piece of bean-shaped greenstone with a piece of chain hanging from it as belonging to her sister. She could not, however, identify the pair of shoes that were then produced in court.

Cohen then tried to establish that Annie Birkett drank heavily, but Lily Nugent answered that her sister would only take a glass of ale, and no, she had never seen her drink whisky.

'Did you know that when she could not get whisky she used to drink methylated spirits?' asked Cohen.

'I am sure that she never did,' answered Mrs Nugent tartly.

'Was she not under the influence of whisky at the wedding ceremony?'

'No.'

'Are you not aware that on the night of the ceremony she had to be put to bed by a woman?'

'No.'

Cohen gave up his attempt to shake her on this point. Lily added that her sister and Crawford had visited her once, and the last time she had seen Annie had been in June or July of 1917, at which time she had visited her sister while she and Crawford were living together.

To further questions from Cohen, Lily replied that the couple did not live happily together, but again denied that this was due to her sister's drinking habits. The accused was not working during the time her sister had had her shop at Balmain. She denied that her sister had a peculiar temperament, and she herself had never had a row with her until she met Crawford.

'What was the row about?' asked Cohen.

'About Crawford. He used to tell yarns. He would tell my sister I said things about her, and tell me she said things about me. I got dissatisfied with Crawford, and felt I could not have him on the place,' replied Lily.

'Did the question of Crawford's sex ever come up?' asked Kidston.

Lily answered no to this.

'He was always a nice man?'

Mrs Nugent made no reply.

The next witness called was Henry (or Harry) Birkett, tailor's apprentice, now living with his aunt at Blakehurst. Birkett (as far as can be judged from the sketch that appeared in *Truth* the following Sunday), was dressed in a neat suit and possessed the same even features as his mother. After going over the events of his mother's and Crawford's life together, he told Kidston that he had last seen his mother in 1917, on the Friday before Eight Hour Day (or Labour Day, in NSW the first Monday in October) in Drummoyne.

That night he got home from work late, and on the following day he went away for the weekend with his employers, the Bones, to Collaroy, and returned on the Monday night.

'I walked through the kitchen and found Crawford sitting at the table,' said Harry. 'He had a glass and a bottle of Johnnie Walker whisky, between half and three quarters full. He looked as if he had been drinking.

'I said, "Where's my mother?"

'He answered, "I don't know."

'I asked him again and he said, "She's gone away with some friends—Mrs Murray and her daughter—to North Sydney." Then I went to bed. He asked me if I would have some whisky and I said "No." In the morning I had my breakfast and went to work. The bottle of whisky was still on the table. It was about a quarter full.'

Kidston: 'Did you notice anything particular about him that morning?'

'No, only he looked as if he had not gone to bed.' The morning after that a boy named George Parnell, whose father worked with Crawford at Perdriau's, came to the house with a bag under his arm, said Harry. He went through the kitchen with Crawford, and Birkett then heard them putting things in the bag. He himself was told nothing of what was happening.

A little later Crawford told him to put on his hat and coat and took him up to Mrs Parnell's, where he was given breakfast. Crawford went away, but returned after about an hour. Then he took him by tram to the railway station, after which they walked to Circular Quay. There Crawford bought two single boat tickets to Watson's Bay, telling him they would return by tram.

At this point, Harry Birkett described a peculiar incident. At Watson's Bay they walked up the hill towards The Gap, he said, and at the edge of the cliff Harry Crawford went outside the two-rail safety fence. Harry Birkett remained inside. Once on the cliff—a common spot for suicide attempts—Crawford started throwing stones over the edge, and he asked young Harry to try as well. Birkett, however, refused to go outside the fence.

'At that time, what was his manner towards you?' asked Kidston.

'He never spoke at all. If I asked anything he would say, "Don't know," or "Come along".' His manner, said Harry Birkett, was unfriendly.

'After that,' continued Birkett, 'he came inside the fence and we walked up to the lighthouse. We came down again into the park, then went back to Sydney by boat. I went to Sargeant's and bought some cakes, and we went through the gardens and we ate them.'

'Did he speak to you?' asked Kidston.

'He seemed to be thinking.'

Harry Birkett added that after tea they went to the house of a Mr Bannon in Glenmore Road. Crawford left him there for the night. He returned next morning with a newspaper, and told him to see if any boys were wanted.

The next day, continued Birkett, Crawford found him a job at Laskers' men's wear in King Street. That night, when he knocked off at 6 p.m., Crawford was waiting for him with 'a young fellow' and the three of them went to a house at 103 Cathedral Street, in the city, where he and Crawford stayed for about a week.

Now Birkett gave evidence of more damning occurrences. One night Crawford had come in with a paper, asking him to see if there was 'anything in it about a murder at North Sydney'. There was a photograph of a pair of shoes in the paper, said Harry, and Crawford, who could neither read nor write, asked if there was any 'reading' about it. Birkett read part of the text, he said, but did not now remember what it was about. Crawford had seemed anxious to know and then took the paper and went into the bedroom.

Nothing had been said about his mother by either of them, said Birkett, and at night Crawford seemed restless. He talked to himself at times. One night they went out, with Crawford carrying a new shovel. It was teeming with rain and there was thunder and lightning. They went from Cathedral Street to Kings Cross, and then took the tram to Ocean Street. From there they walked to Bellevue Road, up the hill and up some stone steps, to a vacant piece of land covered in scrub—he always seemed to follow where Crawford went, the boy added.

Cohen formally objected to this evidence as irrelevant, as these events took place after the death of Annie Birkett. Gale, the Magistrate, said that as the case was going to a higher court he would admit the evidence. It tended to show the state of mind of the accused, he remarked.

Birkett continued that the two of them went to 'a little place in the scrub encircled by trees'. He described how Crawford dug a hole about three feet deep and four feet square, and then asked Birkett to dig. This he did for a while, he said, but then got tired and climbed out, leaving the shovel in the hole. Crawford dug a few more shovelsful and then got out himself. Crawford was taking nips out of a bottle of brandy while Birkett was digging, but he did not speak. Birkett did not ask him what the hole was for. He was tired of asking anything, he told Kidston, because he never got any satisfaction.

They abandoned that hole, and after roaming about the bush for a while, they came to a sandy flat where Crawford again started digging. It was thundering, the lightning was playing, and the rain kept pouring down. Birkett again dug for a while in the shallow hole. Then Crawford told him to stop and throw the shovel into the scrub. They went down the steps and came home, where his landlady, Mrs Schieblich, dried his soaked clothes before the fire. Soon after, they moved to another house.

Next in the stand was Clara Annie Bone, who lived with her husband at Lyons Road, Drummoyne. She had first become acquainted with the Crawford family in 1915, she said. Annie Crawford had done washing for her, and the boy Harry Birkett had run messages for her, and was later employed in her shop. From what she knew, Harry and Annie Crawford appeared to be unhappy together. On 3 October 1917, Harry Crawford had come to her shop and paid his account. He had spoken disrespectfully of his wife, saying she had gone away with another man. Mrs Bone was annoyed with him for taking the boy away, she said. When Crawford told her that Annie had gone away with another man, she said she did not believe it.

In answer to Cohen, Mrs Bone said she had seen the couple out walking on Sundays arm-in-arm, but denied any knowledge concerning Mr Cohen's proposition that they might be going to church.

Ernest Bone, when asked if he had ever heard Harry Crawford using offensive language about his wife, testified: 'Oh yes. One day when we were all down at Five Dock, prawning, I heard him say, "Come here, you long, skinny bastard!"' Another time he referred to the boy Harry as a 'bloody young liar'.

Jane Wigg, of Randwick, who had lived next door to the Crawfords in 1917, stated that she had seen the couple setting out together on the Friday before Eight Hour Day, 1917. Annie Crawford had been wearing a gabardine raincoat and one of them was carrying a small suitcase.

Eliel Irene Carrol, of Longueville, testified that on the Sunday morning before Eight Hour Day, 1917, while on her way to the mills, she had seen a man sitting on a rock with his head buried in his hands. She had seen him again at about 3.30 p.m. the same day.

Answering a question from Cohen, Mrs Carrol said that the look on Crawford's face had frightened her.

'I think the evidence will show the body is that

of Annie Birkett,' the Crown Prosecutor said in conclusion. 'And Falleni was afterwards in a disturbed state of mind.'

The proceedings were adjourned for the day.

Nine

ON THE SECOND DAY of the committal proceedings, Wednesday 18 August, the *Evening News* reported that Miss Marie Tempest, a popular English music hall actress, and her husband and manager Mr Graham Brown, also an actor, had been brought into the court by a private entrance. These 'interested spectators' were escorted across the bench by Mr Gale, the magistrate, and seated adjacent to the solicitors' table in the well of the court. From there they followed the events with great attention.

The inevitable crowd had gathered early to witness the spectacle. The case was this time heard in No. 3 Court, which was usually used to hear marine offences and had no dock. Eugenia, previously shielded from the public gaze by a wooden screen in front of the dock, was now seated on a chair behind the solicitors' table, and hidden by a folding screen of (according to different newspapers) green or blue provided by police authorities. Having been brought into the court before the public was admitted, she was now visible only to the magistrate, the witnesses, and the members of the court. She was again dressed in men's clothes.

When the court adjourned for lunch, the crowd tried

to catch a glimpse of Eugenia as she left. However, she stood behind several police officers, one of whom ordered the people to leave. Eugenia was taken out by the magistrates' entrance.

Much of the day was concentrated on forensic evidence. Sergeant Gorman stated that on 3 October 1917, the day after the finding of the body of the unidentified woman, he had gone to the spot and seen a corked bottle. It had contained about a tablespoon of kerosene. Only a portion of the label remained. The bottle was found about five or six feet from the body, lying under some ashes.

Dr A. A. Palmer, Government Medical Officer, stated that on 3 October 1917 he had examined a badly charred body, of which the features were unrecognisable. There were a number of fissures in the skull, which with one exception might have been caused by the severe heat. The possible exception was a crack in the right side at the back of the head, which might have been due to violence, such as a fall or blow.

In answer to Kidston, Palmer said that there was nothing to show if this crack were caused during life or death. The burning, he believed, had taken place during life.

In answer to Cohen, Palmer said that he had been shown a bottle, and that it had a faint smell of kerosene or methylated spirits, or spirits of some sort, but of what he could not be sure.

Cohen: 'Would it have been possible for a woman to have been drinking and have fallen asleep and then been burnt in the manner this body was burnt?'

'That was my theory at the time,' admitted Palmer.

'You would not say it would be impossible for the

crack on the right side of the head to be caused by intense heat?'

'It may possibly have been.'

It was Kidston's turn. 'Supposing the woman was injured, reduced to unconsciousness, and then burnt, would that be a possible theory of what happened?' he asked.

'Presuming it was due to violence, she would probably have been unconscious at the time. An injury which would produce that fissure would, in many cases, produce unconsciousness,' said Palmer.

Next called was Dr Stratford Sheldon, who corroborated Dr Palmer's evidence. His impression was that the crack on the back of the head was not due to burning. He would not say that it definitely couldn't be, he said, but he didn't think it was.

'We don't have experience of burned bodies every day, but my impression is that it was due to violence,' he concluded.

After the tedium of the preceding hours, the journalists were a little enlivened when Harry Birkett was recalled and shown a copy of the *Evening News* of 16 October 1917, which contained the photograph of the pair of shoes or boots he had identified as his mother's. Harry said that Harry Crawford had got him to read the paper, but he could not remember the date of it. The photograph he saw before him now was similar.

Kidston, reading from the paper, said, 'It was on page three of the issue of...'

Here, one newspaper reported, Cohen shouted, 'I object!' and snatched the newspaper from Kidston's hand. 'He was going to read the date out. I have strong reasons for objecting to it!'

Kidston answered calmly, 'You've got strong hands. I don't know what your reasons are, but there's no reason to resort to violence.'

Gale, the magistrate, admitted the newspaper as evidence.

HENRIETTA SCHIEBLICH, the German landlady from the house in Cathedral Street, was called next. She appeared ill, and a woman friend sat beside her with smelling salts. A German interpreter was sworn in. Mrs Schieblich's evidence was mainly given in English, but the more complicated points, which needed explanation, she made in German to the interpreter.

Mrs Schieblich testified that Harry Crawford and Harry Birkett had stayed in her house at Cathedral Street for thirty shillings a week. His wife had left him, Crawford had told her. Crawford would never let her speak to the boy, and she had never had a chance to ask him if there was anything wrong. Crawford himself spoke sharply to Harry, said Mrs Schieblich, but that was how he spoke generally.

In her broken English, she continued: 'When we read about the woman who was burned he was very excited. He came into the kitchen once and said, "Oh, Mother! Mother! Mother! I don't know. I don't know."' (In some of the newspaper accounts this was given as 'Madame! Madame! Madame!')

'I said, "What's wrong with you?"'

'He sat down at the table, said nothing, and started crying and laughing.'

One morning, said Mrs Schieblich, Crawford came out and said, 'Oh, mother, mother. I am haunted.

The room is haunted.' He was very downhearted and excited, she continued.

'I think your wife is haunting you,' Mrs Schieblich told him. 'I think you killed her.'

Mrs Schieblich claimed to have said this 'only for fun'.

'Oh! Oh! How do you say that for?' Crawford had asked.

'On account of the way you go on,' Mrs Schieblich told him.

'He swore about the boy, and said, "The boy's no good, no good, no good. He's just like his mother. I must get rid of the bugger. He's no good."'

'Did he ever threaten to use any violence towards the boy?' asked Kidston.

'Must I say?'

'Oh, yes.'

'Sometimes he would say, "I am going to kill the—— ".'

Mrs Schieblich offered to look after Harry, she said, but Crawford continued to say the boy was no good and he must get rid of him. She also gave an account of the night on which Crawford took the boy to Bellevue Hill.

One evening when Harry Birkett had got home from work, Crawford borrowed a raincoat from Mr Cross, another boarder, said Mrs Schieblich. It was raining hard, with thunder and lightning. Crawford took a new shovel and went to the gate with Harry. Then he turned back, leaving Harry at the gate, and Mrs Schieblich told him it was pitiful to take the boy out on such a night.

'Did he make any answer?' Kidston asked.

'He opened the door and put his head in and said, "I'm going to kill the—— ." I nearly collapsed, I so upset.'

Mrs Schieblich waited up till they returned home at around ten o'clock, their clothes soaked through and full of sand. She dried the boy's clothes and Crawford said, 'Oh, Harry's a coward. He started crying and would not go to his auntie.' Directly after this, said Mrs Schieblich, Harry Crawford took the boy away.

Mrs Schieblich told the court that Crawford had told her at different times that the boy had received a letter from his mother, who was working in a hotel on the North Shore.

Harry Crawford then also left, but he came back later and said that he had rejoined his wife, but they had had another terrible row and parted again.

Mrs Schieblich had said, 'Bring her to me and I will bring you together again.'

After this, said Mrs Schieblich, Harry Crawford had got absolutely on her nerves, and to get rid of him she had told him that two detectives had been at the house making inquiries.

'And had they?' asked Kidston.

'No, but he was very excited when I told him.' Some articles of women's clothing were produced and Schieblich testified that they were things that Crawford had given her as part payment for his board. According to the newspapers, Cohen then stepped back to where Falleni sat and showed her the articles, and she shook her head several times.

After Crawford had left the house, continued Mrs Schieblich, he had returned to visit occasionally. On one of these occasions she noticed he had had a finger cut off. Twice he brought a lady with him, telling her that this lady was 'very well educated and had money too'.

Cohen asked why, after the incident with the fictitious detectives, Mrs Schieblich had let him live there again.

'Because he was nearly crying when he came to me. He said, "Oh Madame, Madame, Madame, I have no money. I have no one in the world."'

'And although he was as poor as a church mouse, he paid you, didn't he?' asked Cohen.

'Yes.'

Kidston asked Mrs Schieblich if her husband, a violin teacher, drank. The German woman said that Crawford had encouraged her husband to drink Johnnie Walker whisky.

JAMES JABEZ HICKS, orchardist, of Badajoz Road, North Ryde, whom *Truth* sketched as a balding man with a moustache, then testified that in the middle of 1917 he was employed at the Cumberland Paper Mills. On the Sunday before Eight Hour Day of that year, he had seen a man coming from the Lane Cove River towards the mill at about half past five in the morning. When he got to the head of the canal, he stopped, and looked straight towards the spot where the body was afterwards found. He then walked away towards the Chicago Flour Mills. Hicks had identified Falleni as that person. He recognised the walk, he said, and the peculiar swing of the right arm.

Mrs Lydia Parnell, of Cooks Hill, Newcastle, was called. A middle-aged woman wearing a lace collar secured with a brooch, she burst into tears immediately on entering the witness box. She was provided with a chair, and took frequent drinks from a glass of water as she proceeded.

When recovered sufficiently, she gave evidence that in 1917 she had lived in Drummoyne, and knew the accused and Mrs Birkett as Mr and Mrs Crawford. They were an unhappy couple, she said. Harry Crawford told her he had had some trouble with his wife. She did not appear to be satisfied with him, he said, as he was out of work—and in other ways. He said he could not stand the trouble much longer. Something would have to be done.

On the morning after Eight Hour Day, 1917, Harry Crawford carne to her house and seemed upset. He said his wife had not been home all night. She gave him and the boy some breakfast.

When Kidston indicated Eugenia in the dock and asked if Crawford was the person present in the court, Lydia Parnell looked towards Eugenia and almost inaudibly murmured 'Yes.' Then she again broke down in tears. Regaining her composure, Mrs Parnell said that after his wife's disappearance, Crawford was a regular visitor: if he was out of work he stayed with her, and if working he spent his leisure time there.

George William Parnell, Mrs Parnell's son, testified that on one occasion the accused had asked him to read the paper and see if anyone had been found dead or murdered. He read an account of a body being found at Chatswood. For about a week after he was asked by Crawford to read the paper and 'see if there was any more bodies found'.

In answer to a question from Cohen, Parnell said that the accused did not appear to be insane when he asked him to look in the paper.

A witness identified as Emma Belbin testified that she saw the accused 'daily' after meeting him a second time at the Parnell's, and twice he had asked her to write a letter to 'a young lady in the mountains'. Belbin, who did not remember the name of the young lady in question, said she had written the letters in March 1918.

Kidston asked if she remembered the terms of those letters. Cohen objected, and Kidston did not press.

The proceedings were adjourned to the next day.

Ten

A LITTLE OVER A MONTH before, Josephine Falleni, Eugenia's daughter, had been found and brought to Police Headquarters, where detectives Robson and Watkins interviewed her at length and with all their considerable expertise. Although apprehensive and in ill-health, at this stage Josephine seemed quite forthcoming in her information to the officers. A transcript of Josephine's statement was printed in a number of newspapers in incomplete form, with some newspapers supplying details left out by others.

As far back as Josephine could remember, she had told police, she had been going under the name of 'De Anglis'. Brought up by Mrs De Anglis (or De Angelis)—whom she called Grannie—at Pelham Street, she had been sent to school at five, first to Double Bay Public School and later to St Joseph's Roman Catholic School, Woollahra, which she had left at twelve. She could first remember her mother when she was about seven years old, she said. Her mother used to visit them often; she always wore men's clothing and was known as Harry Crawford. Mrs De Anglis used to carry on a laundry business, and her mother worked for her, driving the cart and delivering laundry.

Mr De Anglis would tell his wife that if she did not get rid of the baby (meaning herself) he would leave her and go back to Italy, said Josephine. Grannie refused, and Mr De Anglis returned to Rome and, Josephine understood, had died there. Mrs De Anglis had told her that Harry Crawford was her mother, and her father was a captain of a boat. Mrs De Anglis also told her that she was born at her house at Double Bay. The statement continued:

> My mother was very cruel to me when
> [I was] a child, and used to frighten me.
> On many occasions she used to try to take
> me away from Grannie, and Grannie of-
> ten told me my mother tried to smother
> me when I was a baby. My mother used to
> work for Grannie for a while, then leave
> her, and return in a few months. She used
> to quarrel with her a great deal. I lived
> with Grannie until I was about fourteen
> years of age, and then my Grannie died.

Her mother had then called for her at Double Bay, Josephine said, and asked if she had any money. When Josephine said no, she told her she would take her away with her to Balmain. This was late in 1914. Her mother, said Josephine, took her to a little confectionery shop in Darling Street, Balmain, at about twelve o'clock one night. The shop was kept by Mrs Birkett, who had a son named Harry about thirteen years of age.

> My mother told me that Mrs Birkett had

> some money, and that Mrs Birkett always
> thought that mother was a man. I said to
> my mother one day, 'She will find you out
> one of these days.' My mother said, 'Oh,
> I'll watch it. I would rather do away with
> myself than let the police find out anything
> about me.' Shortly after that, I think it was
> next day, my mother took me to live with
> a Mrs Keith in Hoffman's Lane, in Balmain.
> At this time I had some trouble, and later on
> I went to St Margaret's Home. My mother
> used to visit me there, and also afterwards.

Josephine (who was referring to her pregnancy here) went back to Mrs Birkett's some time later, she said. Her mother told her always to call her 'father', and not to let Mrs Birkett or anyone else know that she was a woman. She did not think her mother was married to Mrs Birkett. 'My mother always used to call Mrs Birkett "Daisy",' said Josephine, 'and she called my mother "Harry".'

Her mother and Mrs Birkett used to occupy the same bedroom, she continued, and she always called her mother 'father'.

> She and Mrs Birkett used to quarrel a lot,
> and my mother would say to me, 'More
> rows over you.' I answered my mother,
> and she said, 'A lovely daughter I've got,'
> and I said, 'Yes, and a lovely mother I've
> got.' She took a silk shawl from me and
> gave it to Mrs Birkett as a present.

In 1917 Josephine left Mrs Birkett's house and went to live in Kent Street so as to be near to her work. While working at Parson Bros. as a packer she went out to see her mother at Drummoyne, but no one was home. She was told at a grocer shop that they did not know where her mother was.

> I later met my mother and she told me not to go and see Mrs Birkett as she would 'go' for me. She also said, 'Everything is unsettled and upside down. Daisy has found out that I am a woman. I am going my way and Daisy is going her way.'
>
> I said to my mother, 'Who has got the jewellery?' My mother said, 'Oh, she has got all that.' I forget the date, but that was in 1917, and my mother seemed very agitated and upset. A few weeks later I met my mother, who said she was living at Annandale.
>
> I said, 'Where is Mrs Birkett?' She replied, 'I don't know, I think she is in service.'

Josephine remembered reading in a newspaper about a woman's death and about a body found at Chatswood at about this time. She had asked her mother if she thought the woman found was Daisy. To this her mother replied, 'Oh, she might have got rid of herself. She drank a lot.' Josephine's statement concluded:

> I have only seen my mother on a few occasions since that date, when I met her in the

street a few times. She never wanted to speak to me. I said to her on one occasion, 'Where is Harry?' She replied, 'Oh, she has left him with me—what am I going to do with him?' My mother used to smoke a lot and drink a great deal of whisky. She was always reticent about herself and would tell me very little.
[Signed] Josephine Crawford.

NOW, on the third day of the committal proceedings, Thursday 19 August, a very frightened Josephine Falleni was brought forward as the principal witness. Sobbing, she was led into the court by an attendant, and given a seat in front of the witness box, in full view of the curiosity seekers. The *Evening News* noted that she was smartly dressed in a dark blue costume trimmed with fur, a small black hat, and a grey motor veil. This last she carefully kept down over her face all the time, so that her features were invisible. She sobbed all the time she was giving her answers, making her replies difficult to understand. *Truth* added to this the information that the hat was trimmed with imitation fruit, the suit was serge, and her stockings were of blue silk.

The fact that Josephine was completely hidden by a veil apparently did not stop *Truth* artist from making a clumsy sketch of her, in which she seemed to have inherited her mother's strong jaw, but otherwise appeared as an attractive young woman. The *Sun* of 19 August noted that Josephine did not once look at her mother during the proceedings. Her responses to Kidston were in sharp contrast to her previous statement, and evasive in the extreme. They were also reproduced in great detail by the newspapers.

Josephine gave her full name as Josephine Crawford Falleni, and her address as Harris Street, Pyrmont. The first she remembered of her mother was her coming to visit the house where she was brought up, she said.

'When did you first meet Mrs Birkett?' asked Kidston.

'I can't remember,' Josephine replied.

'She had a son?'

'Yes, but I have no idea at all how old he was.'

'You always knew your mother was a woman?'

'Yes.'

'She went about in men's clothes?'

'Yes.'

'When did Mrs Birkett find out the accused was a woman?'

'I don't know. She never told me anything about her business.'

'Did your mother ever say anything about the police?'

'No.'

'When did Mrs Birkett and your mother live together as husband and wife?'

'At the shop at Balmain.'

'What did you call your mother?'

'I never used to call her anything at all.'

'Did she tell you what to call her in Mrs Birkett's presence?'

'No.'

'Did you see if they occupied the same bedroom?'

'Yes. The same room and the same bed.'

'What terms were they on? Did they have rows?'

'They used to have rows over me.'

'What terms were you on with your mother?'
'Not very good terms.'
'Did you go to your mother's place at Drummoyne?'
'Yes. Mrs Crawford was there.'
'Did your mother ever tell you about Mrs Crawford finding out she was a woman?'
'She never told me.'
'Did you ever tell anybody in your mother's presence, that your mother was a woman, or that Mrs Crawford would find it out?'

Mr Gale, the magistrate, at this point interrupted the dialogue to say, 'Her mother would naturally be a woman.'

Kidston rephrased the question. 'Did you ever tell anybody in your mother's presence that your mother was a woman, dressed in men's clothes?'

'I don't remember.'
'Did you ever ask your mother about Mrs Crawford's jewellery?'
'No.'
'Do you remember the last time you saw Mrs Crawford?'
'No. I don't remember.'
'Did your mother ever tell you Mrs Crawford had disappeared?'
'No.'
'Do you remember reading in the paper about a body being found in the bush at Chatswood?'
'Yes.'
'Do you remember your mother telling you anything about it?'
'I forget now.'
'Did you ever remember?'

'I don't remember at all.'
'Did you ever remember?'
'No, I did not.'
'Do you think you will ever remember?'

The prosecutor was obviously becoming irritated with this unproductive encounter, and Cohen broke in with an objection, which was supported by Gale.

'We can't have that, Mr Kidston,' the magistrate rebuked him.

Kidston resumed his examination of Josephine in gentler tones, but Josephine continued to claim she could not remember. When Kidston asked if her mother ever drank, again Josephine answered evasively.

'Not in company. I never saw her under the influence of drink in company.'

But by now the prosecutor had had enough.

'Did you ever make a statement to the police?' he asked.

'Yes,' answered Josephine.

Cohen objected, and Gale told Kidston he could have that fact and nothing further.

The prosecutor produced a copy of the document and demanded that Josephine look at the signature.

'Yes, I did sign that,' Josephine responded.

'That is your signature to the statement you made to the police?' repeated Kidston.

'Yes.'

'Before you signed it, it was read over to you?'

'Yes, by Detective Robson.'

'Were you satisfied that it was correct?'

Cohen again objected, and Gale upheld the objection.

Now Cohen began his questioning of the witness, somewhat more kindly.

'In what condition of mind were you when you signed that statement?'

'I was too upset.'

'Did you understand what Detective Robson was reading at the time?'

'I was too upset and sick of it all,' Josephine repeated.

Cohen changed tack. 'Do you remember getting a letter from me asking you to come to my office?'

'Yes,' the girl answered.

'Did you take that letter to the Police Department?'

'Yes.'

'And did they advise you not to go?'

'Yes.'

To further questioning from Maddocks Cohen, Josephine testified that she had lived at Drummoyne with her mother and Mrs Birkett. Mrs Birkett had complained that she did not get enough money from her, and that she came home too late at night.

Cohen: 'Have you ever seen her drink?'

'Yes, beer.'

'Have you seen her take whisky?'

'No, but I've smelt it on her. She used to smash up things when she was like that.'

'You remember on one occasion—' began Cohen, but at this point Kidston objected to Cohen breaking new ground in his cross-examination.

Gale commented that it was quite evident that Josephine was now giving evidence willingly, where she was unwilling before.

'The poor girl is in a trying position,' he said, 'and I am sorry for her.'

In answer to further questions Josephine said that Mrs Birkett often broke crockery during rows. Her mother stuck up for her on these occasions, she said, and Mrs Birkett fought against her. She earned only seventeen shillings a week, and could not give any more board than she was already doing.

By this time, Josephine was again in tears, and when Kidston resumed his questioning, Gale interrupted to say that he thought they would adjourn for lunch, to give the witness a chance to pull herself together. Kidston told him that Josephine had been crying for three days, and he did not think the situation would improve.

After the adjournment, Kidston attempted to continue his questioning, but again Josephine could not control her sobbing.

The prosecutor told the magistrate that in view of Miss Falleni's attitude he wanted her treated as a hostile witness. Cohen objected to this, arguing that the witness was visibly distressed and had answered to the best of her ability. The questions he had himself put to her were entirely different to those put by Mr Kidston, he added.

'Will you read the last part of your signed statement?' Kidston asked Josephine. Once more Cohen objected, but was overruled.

When shown the statement Josephine said she could not read it through her veil, and would not lift her veil to read it. Kidston surmounted the difficulty by putting the document under her veil.

'You said this morning you never saw your mother drunk?' he asked.

'Yes.'

Kidston again asked for permission to table the signed statement. He addressed the court. 'In the report she signed she stated: "My mother used to smoke a lot and drink a good deal of whisky. She often smelt a lot of whisky."'

Turning to Josephine, he asked, 'Did you say that?'

'Yes,' admitted Josephine.

Gale granted permission to table the statement. 'I'm satisfied that the girl does not want to say anything to injure her mother,' he said.

Kidston tabled the document, and asked Josephine if she had made a statement relative to her mother's drinking which was contrary to her evidence. Josephine admitted that she had.

Kidston repeated his request that Josephine be treated as a hostile witness. He would not ask her any further questions on the subject, he said, but would treat her as humanely as possible. Gale agreed to the request.

Josephine told Kidston that Cohen did not know what evidence she had been going to give. She had gone to the detectives' office, she said, but not to Mr Cohen's.

Kidston stated that he would ask the witness no more questions, so as not to distress her.

Further examined by Cohen, Josephine said that she saw a Dr Gibbes two days after she had made the statement. She had previously told Kidston that Detective Robson had been kind to her when she made the statement—she had been sick at the time, and he had taken her to the doctor. Ever since the detectives had come for her, she maintained, she had been in bad health. The answers she had given that morning were absolutely true, she said.

Josephine was dismissed.

Detective Robson submitted as evidence Eugenia Falleni's statement made at the time of her arrest on 5 July of that year. At the end of the session, Eugenia was committed for trial.

Eleven

MORAN, in his account of Eugenia, seemed conversant with all the testimony as it was presented in the press, and appeared to have access to other information as well. In one instance he referred to 'unpublished records of the case', which apparently dealt with testimony about aspects of Eugenia's personal relationships.

The doctor also mentioned W. T. Coyle, the Crown Prosecutor, a lifelong friend and correspondent, and perhaps he was a source of information. Moran, in addition, had the benefit of his conversations with Eugenia in prison.

Dr Moran had to be taken on trust as a writer with a scientific respect for accuracy, but I found myself wondering how much his account was influenced by the myth or rumour that seemed to have grown up around the case. Eugenia had presented the police with several highly fictitious versions of her own life, and would, at a later date, perhaps present a similarly unreliable story to Moran. I wondered if, in the final reckoning, what Eugenia believed about herself might also prove fictitious.

Although by now a number of the original 'givens' of

Moran's account had faded into uncertainty through errors and contradictions in the various extant accounts, the original conundrum still existed. The obvious motive for the alleged murder, and the one supported by Moran—Eugenia's fear of betrayal of her secret—had never seemed a strong one to me because of the eight or nine months that had apparently elapsed between Annie Birkett's discovery of Harry's true sex and her death. This was the weak point in the theory. If such a betrayal did not provoke an immediate reaction, why should it provoke such a reaction eight months later? What threat was posed by Annie that had not been posed before?

More to the point, why murder? Why did not Harry Crawford simply disappear, change his name once more, and resume his life elsewhere? What had happened in the preceding months that now made Annie's death so imperative? And even given that something had happened to precipitate a crisis, the conclusion that Annie's death was a result of murder did not necessarily seem proven. A defence of manslaughter, even of accidental death, still seemed tenable. If Eugenia Falleni did kill Annie Birkett, it was, strictly speaking, against the odds. According to all the statistics, women seldom commit murder; more rarely still do they kill other women; and even more rarely do they do it by violent means.

The trial transcript, I hoped, might answer some of these questions.

EUGENIA FALLENI stood trial on Tuesday 5 October 1920 in the Central Criminal Court of New South Wales at Darlinghurst before Chief Justice Sir

William Cullen and a jury of twelve. Mr W. T. Coyle, KC, appeared for the Crown, instructed by Mr John Gonsalves of the Crown Law Department. Mr A. McDonnell, instructed by Mr Maddocks Cohen, appeared for the defence. Sixteen witnesses were called on the first day. The Crown would call, over the next two days, a total of 27 witnesses. The defence would call one. Of the court records of the case held in the Archives Office of New South Wales, the Crown witnesses' testimony would cover 85 typed sheets; the testimony for the defence, and the accused's statement on her own behalf, three.

The *Sun* newspaper of that day reported that many of the women who had gathered hours before were disappointed at not being allowed into the court to witness the proceedings. About thirty women gained admittance to the imposing sandstone courthouse at Taylor Square, and the upper gallery, which allowed only men and held about ninety people, was filled. Many of the male spectators were nineteen- and twenty-year-old youths.

Eugenia had been given the option of appearing in male or female attire, the paper claimed, and she appeared in the dock slightly before 10 a.m. wearing, for the first time in public, women's clothing. This consisted of a white linen blouse with a big, squarish collar turned out over a black woollen coat, a white skirt, and black buttoned boots with brown cloth tops. On her head was a black velvet hat with a brim. Her hair, brushed back, barely touched her collar. As she walked towards the dock, reported the *Evening News*, there were exclamations of disappointment that she was not dressed as a man.

Once she was seated, the crowd in the galleries were prevented from seeing her by the position of the dock. She spoke calmly with her solicitor before the Chief Justice took his seat.

Advised by her solicitor Mr McDonnell, Eugenia exercised her right of challenge very freely, and altogether challenged eleven jurors as they were called. These, according to the *Sun*, were in the majority bearded, old or grey-haired men. Coyle, for the Crown, challenged one, before the final twelve were settled on. As was customary, all the jurors were male. The reporter from the *Daily Telegraph* of the same day wrote that Falleni was pale and nervous during these preliminaries, but regained her composure as the Crown Prosecutor outlined the case—a composure that the reporter described as 'unusual in murder trials'. Sometimes, said the paper, she cast furtive and anxious glances around the court.

The charge was read. Having been asked to plead, Eugenia replied in a low but distinct voice, 'Not guilty', then stood with her hands clasped low in front of her and her mouth shut tightly.

Coyle, in his opening address, told the court that Eugenia Falleni was known as 'the man-woman' because she had for years dressed as a man and undertaken a man's work in factories and other places. In 1913, while masquerading as a man, she had gone through a form of marriage at Balmain with Annie Bell Birkett, a widow. At that time she had assumed the name of Harry Leon Crawford and given Florence as her birthplace. Annie Birkett, said Coyle (erroneously), had been married in 1910, and had one child, Harry Birkett, who was now seventeen.

This unfortunate woman, who was known as Mrs Crawford, had disappeared in September 1917, continued Coyle. Charred remains found a little later at Chatswood were subsequently identified as hers. It was for the murder of Mrs Crawford, as she was called, that the accused was now on trial.

The Crown would show, said Coyle, that the accused and Annie Birkett had frequently quarrelled in 1917, and that the accused was violent in language and manner. The remains were found by chance on 2 October 1917, in the bush near Mowbray Road, Chatswood. The accused was not charged with the murder until July of this year. It had been discovered that she had a daughter in Sydney, Miss Falleni, a young woman who appeared to be familiar with her mother's way of living. While the post mortem examination on the remains of the deceased Annie Birkett—Mrs Crawford—failed to detect any marks of violence, the Crown would maintain that the fire that had caused the woman's death was not an accident. In the opinion of Dr Palmer, the Government medical officer who conducted the post mortem, Annie Birkett was alive when her clothing caught fire or was set on fire. The accused had been seen on and before 28 September 1917 in the vicinity of the bush where the remains were found.

Coyle rapidly summarised the details of Harry and Annie's life together until September 1917. The jury would hear from Harry Bell Birkett, Annie Birkett's son, that on 28 September, the Friday before Eight Hour Day, Annie Crawford had got his breakfast before he went to work, and that was the last time her son saw her.

The prosecutor then switched to the statement of another inhabitant of The Avenue, Drummoyne, where the couple had been living. This woman would testify that on the Friday before Eight Hour Day she saw the accused and the woman she knew as Mrs Crawford—the dead woman—going out, one of them carrying a small suitcase.

Coyle added that there was a tram running from Drummoyne towards Ryde, which branched off towards the Lane Cove River at the Gladesville mental asylum. A little over a mile or two from the tram line, past many quiet and unfrequented spots, were the Cumberland Paper Mills, and a little further on the Chicago Flour Mills, where the accused had once worked.

He referred to the evidence of a Mrs Carrol, who on the same Friday had seen a man sitting with his head in his hands near the paper mills—a man so highly excited and strung up that, as she approached him, he jumped. This man Mrs Carrol had identified as the accused. Coyle then moved on to the evidence of two men who, near the mills between 5.30 and 7.30 a.m. on the Sunday, had seen a stranger whom they noticed particularly because strangers were rare at that time of the morning. Both also noticed that he looked up the hill in the direction that the body was later found.

Like Mrs Carrol, both had this year been able to identify this person as the accused.

The Crown would argue, said Coyle, that on the Friday, at the time of Mrs Carrol's sighting, the accused, who was observably nervous and jumpy, had already left Annie Birkett dead within 400 yards of the top of the hill.

When Hicks and Woodbury had seen him on Sunday, Coyle continued, the accused, perhaps unable to get rid of something, had returned to the same place.

Coyle mentioned the forensic evidence, and the Government medical officers' opinion that one of a number of cracks in the skull had been caused by violence rather than heat. He admitted, however, that they were not prepared to say that the crack could not have been caused by the fire.

The prosecutor now moved on to the assortment of objects found on and near the body, including the false teeth, and claimed that these constituted proof that the body was that of Annie Birkett.

After Mrs Birkett's disappearance, Coyle continued, Harry Crawford had told another person that his wife had 'bolted with a plumber from Balmain'. He told someone else that his wife had 'cleared out without leaving him a penny'; and to another he said that they had had many rows, and that he 'had to do something'.

During that week their household effects were packed up, and Harry made arrangements to sell them. The man who bought the furniture, noticing the accused's demeanour, had asked if Harry's wife consented to the sale. Harry assured him that his wife knew all about it and had no objection, and that she was over in North Sydney.

'She was over in North Sydney, gentlemen,' Coyle pronounced ominously. 'That is the only true thing that the accused has said.'

So this, concluded the prosecutor, was the story of the events of September and October 1917. Since then the boy had grown older, things had been said, and the whole had culminated in the arrest of the accused in July of this year. When arrested, the accused had made a statement that was a tissue of lies.

Coyle said that he would speak now on another matter—although, he added, it was an unpleasant subject on which to speak in front of the women present. Here the Chief Justice interrupted to comment that if women chose to come to a criminal court, their feelings need not be considered.

Harry Crawford had been through the form of marriage with a woman, said Coyle, and the Crown maintained that in this lay a motive for getting rid of Annie Birkett. It was only when his deceit was discovered that there were quarrels between the two, and that Harry sought an opportunity to get rid of the person who might broadcast that deceit.

While the post-mortem examination on the remains of the deceased failed to detect any marks of violence, Coyle repeated, the Crown would ask the jury to find that the fire which caused the woman's death was not accidental. According to medical opinion, Annie Birkett had been alive when her clothing caught fire or was set alight. And the accused had been seen on or before 28 September near where the charred remains were found.

'All her actions since then,' finished Coyle, 'have been characterised by cunning and deceit.'

Twelve

COYLE, after his opening address to the jury, produced his formidable array of witnesses. A significant proportion of the prosecution's time was taken up with the identification by these witnesses of objects that would help to establish that Annie Birkett and the woman found in the bush were the same person. These exhibits included marriage certificates, photographs of Annie Birkett and her son, the things found in the ashes of the fire, and various of Annie's possessions.

Lily Nugent, Annie's sister, who said she was now living with her husband at Kogarah, was sworn in first. Questioned at length by Coyle, she reiterated that she had known the accused as Harry Crawford for seven or eight years, and had witnessed her sister's wedding. In early 1917, she said, she had discovered that Crawford was not a man.

In her next answers Mrs Nugent inadvertently began to refer to Eugenia as 'he', at which the Chief Justice broke in with a query as to whom she meant. Similar confusion continued throughout the trial, with Eugenia at various times being referred to as 'he', 'she', and in one instance at least (when a medical witnesses was at a loss) 'it'.

Lily Nugent had seen her sister only twice during 1917, she said, and after the first time, not in the presence of the accused. (Here Lily said, 'I never saw him again after I knew that he was a man,' which, being queried by the Chief Justice, she amended to, 'I mean I never saw her again after I knew she was a woman.')

Her sister had come to see her in about January 1917, Lily continued, after writing to her to say that she had something she wanted to tell her. Crawford was with her, but he was not present when she made her disclosure. She had not seen him again until this year.

Mr Archibald McDonnell—unmarried at 52, a neat man with a walrus moustache—began his cross-examination of Lily by asking about Falleni's behaviour at the wedding. Mrs Nugent said that Falleni had not been under the influence of liquor on the day, but her sister and Falleni had seen her off on the ten o'clock train, so she could not account for what happened after that. She, Lily, had had two babies at the time, and her sister had carried one. Before the marriage she and her sister had always been friendly.

After the marriage they were still friendly, she said, but Crawford had made mischief. In 1914 she had an argument with him and a dispute with her sister.

Lily Nugent did not know which of the couple appeared to be more attached, she told McDonnell. When Annie had left her place to work for Dr Binns, Crawford would visit her there. He pestered her. In her opinion, said Lily, he was more anxious to continue in her sister's company than her sister was in his.

HARRY BELL BIRKETT, Annie Birkett's son, had known Harry Crawford some years, he told the prosecutor, having first met him at Dr Clarke's, where Crawford was a useful and gardener. He had been eleven or twelve when his mother bought the shop at Balmain, and Crawford was always hanging around and bothering her. He came every day and every evening, and eventually she was forced to marry him. After that, Crawford had come to live with them. Six months later his mother sold the business, and he and she went to live at Kogarah. Harry Crawford did not then come with them.

When his mother went to work for Dr Binns, however, he came every Saturday, bothering her again. In the end his mother had to leave, and they went to live in Austral Street. From there they went to No. 7, and then to No. 5, The Avenue, Drummoyne. This was about 1915. Crawford worked at Perdriau's as, Harry understood, a tyre repairer, and his mother went out to do housework. After Harry left school in 1916, he went to work for Mrs Bone at the grocery shop, for whom he had previously run messages. He would leave for work between eight and eight-thirty in the morning. On Saturdays, as his mother sometimes slept in, he would get his own breakfast, but on weekdays his mother did.

The last time he had seen his mother was on the Friday morning before Eight Hour Day, when his mother made him breakfast before work, he told Coyle. On Friday nights he usually ate at Bone's, the grocer's, as he worked late, and did not come home until ten or half past. That Friday he returned at ten at night and did not see anybody, and so went straight to bed. He could not definitely remember getting his own breakfast next morning, but he presumed that he had. He went to work, had lunch at Mrs Bone's and, after coming home to change his clothes, went with her and her family to Collaroy beach for the weekend.

Coyle questioned Birkett repeatedly as to whether he had got his own breakfast that morning, but the boy continued to maintain that he could not remember. He had seen no one when he came home to change, he said. The front door had been open. He thought that his mother might have been at a neighbour's place, so he had got his clothes and gone away.

When he returned on Monday evening at half past eight, Harry Birkett reiterated, as he had in the Police Court, that the front door was again open and he had walked in, finding Crawford in the kitchen drinking whisky.

Coyle continued leading Harry Birkett through the events of the next two days, including his breakfast at Mrs Parnell's and the packing of the furniture, until, on the Tuesday night, Crawford had taken him by ferry from Circular Quay to The Gap at Watson's Bay. When he reached the point of describing how Crawford had gone outside the safety fence, McDonnell objected, and Coyle did not press the question.

Harry Birkett was allowed to state that they were some little time at The Gap, and returned from there by ferry. He described staying the night at Mr Bannon's at Glenmore Road. After this, he said, perhaps a week after he had last seen his mother, he had found a job and gone to live at Cathedral Street, where he shared a room with Crawford.

Harry Crawford swore and called his mother all sorts of things when they quarrelled, using filthy language, he told Coyle. He had never seen his mother not sober, and had seen Crawford drunk only about twice.

Coyle now led him through his evidence concerning Crawford's asking him to read the *Evening News*, in which there was a photograph of a pair of patched shoes, and about Crawford's subsequent behaviour. A newspaper was produced, which Harry Birkett identified as similar to the one in question.

Birkett also identified a pair of shoes as his mother's property. The patches were similar to those often done by Crawford, using floor tacks, or anything he could get hold of. In turn he identified as his mother's property an enamel cup, a hat pin, the chain and locket found in the ashes, and a brooch. Some pieces of cloth shown to him were similar to that of his mother's clothing, he said, and he also identified as hers a small trunk, a diamond ring, a broken bottle with the word 'Robert' on the glass, a drinking glass and a jacket.

After he left 103 Cathedral Street, he had gone to live with a Mrs Bombelli at 156 Cathedral Street, said Harry Birkett, and Crawford often came there. Birkett himself subsequently went with Frank Bombelli, Mrs Bombelli's son, to live at Sans Souci.

McDonnell, in his cross-examination, initially concentrated on Harry Birkett's relationship with Crawford. It was not as good as it should have been, Harry Birkett admitted. Crawford treated him abruptly, and he had as little to do with him as possible. He swore at the boy frequently, but did not chastise or beat him. His mother had supplied most of his clothes and food with the money she brought home. On the occasions he had come to the Bombelli's, Crawford had not spoken to him, but had talked in Italian to Mrs Bombelli.

In other evidence, Birkett said that while his mother had been working for Dr Binns at Kogarah, Crawford had come to see her on a Saturday afternoon, sometimes on a Sunday. His mother would complain that he was pestering her. It was his mother who had engaged the house at Austral Street. When they went there they had no furniture, but his mother had gone to Woolworths' sale rooms and bought some. All this was paid for by his mother, as in the first two or three months Crawford was not working.

After this, said Harry Birkett, they had moved to Drummoyne. Crawford had been working at Perdriau's, and at that time was supporting the house. Harry Birkett understood that his mother had paid between £80 and £90 for the shop in Balmain, and had had to sell it for about £25.

After a few more questions, Harry Birkett retired as a witness.

DR ARTHUR AUBREY PALMER, Government Medical Officer, was called to testify that on 2 October 1917 he had, with ex-Superintendent Tait, examined the charred remains of a woman near the Cumberland Paper Mills at Lane Cove. On 3 October 1917 he had seen the same remains at the City Morgue, he said, and these were the same remains that were submitted to him from a coffin on 22 July this year, 1920.

Dr Palmer's testimony in answer to Coyle, and his subsequent cross-examination by McDonnell, continued until the luncheon adjournment, and then recommenced. By the length of the transcribed evidence, Dr Palmer was on the stand for one and a half hours, and Dr Sheldon after him for another twenty minutes. Both doctors' testimony was chiefly concerned with the forensic evidence, much of which was detailed in scientific terms and would have presented some difficulties for the lay jurors.

Together with Dr Stratford Sheldon, said Palmer, he had examined the body, which was very much burned. The features were unrecognisable, the ribs burnt through and the internal organs cooked. The legs were not burnt below the knee, and at the junction of the burned and unburned portions there were large, fluid-filled blisters surrounded by red skin. From the blistering Palmer had concluded that the body had been burnt during life, but whether conscious or not he could not say.[4]

In the cavities of the body, including mouth, chest, abdomen and vagina, there were maggots. The legs showed no marked signs of decomposition. Palmer had concluded that the body had been there no longer than two days, judging by the size of the maggots and the condition of the legs.

The tissues of the head were charred. They had removed the skull cap and examined the brain, which

---

4   Palmer's and Sheldon's evidence that the fluid-filled blisters on Annie Birkett's body indicated that she was alive at the time her body was burned—leading to the unlikely scenario that she may have lain unconscious for three days before Harry Crawford returned to set fire to her body—has since been discredited. On this point, Mark Tedeschi, in his book *Eugenia* (Simon and Schuster, Sydney 2012, pp. 229, 259 (Chapter 30, note 1) cites the opinion of Dr Rebecca Irvine, Forensic Pathologist at Glebe Corner's Court.

was cooked. They had looked for obvious fractures in the skull, and lesions, but, at the time, did not go beyond that. The fact that there were no evident effusions of blood—although little would be evident after such burning—had led them to believe at the time that there was no fracture, although they knew that if they had removed the charred flesh from the bones, fissures caused by the burning would probably be found. But this was impossible in an ordinary post-mortem.

On 21 July of this year, 1920 (here Dr Palmer, with permission, referred to his notes) a coffin was brought to the morgue and opened in his and Dr Edwards' presence. He had assisted Dr Edwards in taking X-ray photographs for the detection of any metallic substance such as bullets. (Here seven photographs were tendered and marked as exhibits.)

On 22 July, with Dr Sheldon, he again examined the body and took more photographs. On this second examination, he found that all the charred parts of the body had disintegrated. The uncharred parts had also disintegrated into a substance known as adipocere; a greasy, fatty material. Now the skull was quite bare, as were the ribs and the spinal column. The adipocere separated quite easily from the bones of the unburnt sections, so that in effect they could examine the entire skeleton.

They examined the bones of the skull by X-ray, and found at least seven fissures or cracks or breaks. Six of these were due to heat, and were what he would have expected to find. They were in thin bone, such as the face, where heat could pass into the sinus and expand.

There was also another crack, a linear crack through

the thick portion at the back of the skull on the right hand side—Dr Palmer, with permission, demonstrated on his own head—about two and a half inches long. Both doctors saw it at the same time, and both, said Palmer, thought it was undoubtedly due to violence. The skull itself was more severely burnt than they had expected.

Here Dr Palmer reached into his bag and—rather bizarrely—produced Annie Birkett's actual skull in court, with the skull cap removed, and demonstrated the frontal cracks, which he said he believed were due to the fire, and the posterior one, which both doctors now believed was due to violence.

McDonnell, in his cross-examination, reminded Palmer that he had said at the Coroner's Court that they had found no definite marks of violence. Palmer confirmed this. It was only on further examination, and consultation with other doctors, that they had discovered this new evidence, he maintained. He still believed that death had been due to burning, although the woman had no appearance of having been set on fire deliberately.

McDonnell, for the Defence, invoked a lengthy and detailed repetition of the earlier evidence concerning the blisters, and Palmer's conclusion, which Palmer still held, that the woman had been alive at the time of the burning. Palmer finished by admitting that it was possible that the natural fuel provided by the scrub could have contributed to causing the seventh crack, but that he doubted it.

Questioned by Sir Edward Cullen, Palmer stated that he was not prepared to give a definite opinion on the matter.

McDonnell continued to pursue the point, asking whether concentrated heat on a thick portion of the skull might tend to produce a linear crack (such as might be caused by violence) rather than a stellate (or star-shaped) one like the others. Again Palmer answered at length, touching on the composition of bones and the relationship of the bones of the skull to each other, and their tendencies to different types of cracking with the application of heat. He referred to *Halliburton's Handbook of Physiology* of 1904, which he said he took as correct on these matters.

Palmer once again confirmed that his original opinion had been that the woman had possibly been drinking, had fallen asleep, and had been accidentally burnt. That was his theory at the time, he said. The body was close to the fire, it did not seem to have been moved, there was no sign of a struggle and no obvious blood. This was the evidence he had given at the inquest at the Coroner's Court, at the Police Court, and he reconfirmed having given it now.

It was generally accepted that women and children burned more readily than men, he commented. This was due to their clothing being flimsier and more voluminous, and because of the layers of air between.

When the court was adjourned for lunch, to recommence at 2.00 p.m., Eugenia, under charge of a wardress, had her meal in a room adjoining the court. Afterwards she returned quickly to the dock, where, according to the newspapers, she paid close attention to the evidence.

Palmer, still responding to questions from McDonnell, repeated that although after exhumation the fractures to the skull were very much more visible than at the earlier examination, no fresh cracks would have appeared. He could not say for sure that there had been no marks of violence on other parts of the body as it had been too badly burnt.

Palmer had been shown a bottle, which he smelt, he agreed, and identified it as the one shown in evidence now. It had been suggested at the time that the bottle had smelt of kerosene, and he had replied, 'Perhaps it does'—or words to that effect. He had suggested it be sent to the Government Analyst. The bottle had had some smell, he said, but he had been unsure what it was.

After another series of questions on the nature of cracks caused by fire and violence, McDonnell changed tack. Dr Palmer responded to McDonnell's next question by stating that during the last fifty years a very large body of literature had grown up with reference to sexual inversion. He did not have a great knowledge of it himself, he said, although he had read constantly of it. In some cases the sexual instincts of a man were implanted in a woman, although the sexual organs were those of a woman, and childbearing was not impaired. On the other hand, he said, there were men with the sexual organ of a man, and otherwise the physical attributes of a woman.

Here McDonnell produced a book, described as being by a Professor Talbot, and showed it to Palmer, who was not prepared to say if the picture therein represented a man or a woman. It was a bad photograph, he commented.

On the next page, continued Palmer in response to McDonnell, there was a figure with sloping shoulders. This could possibly indicate a female skeleton, but he would not like to draw any conclusion from that. One saw all sorts of variations in the sexes that were without any inversion at all. He would not rely on physical formation any more than he would on the old idea of diagnosing criminals from appearance.

McDonnell asked another question (undisclosed in the transcript), to which Coyle objected. There followed an inconclusive exchange about embryology and cell differentiation, and at what stage of development sexual characteristics appeared.

McDonnell moved on to ask whether it was not a fact that, given that there were men who were more or less feminine and women who were more or less masculine, the degree of the tendency to have the sexual impulse of the opposite sex might vary from one per cent to almost complete? Palmer agreed that he believed this was so.

McDonnell now asked if it were not the case that even when a person had an impulse in the direction of his or her own sex, the organs of that person were usually complete. Palmer replied that he thought in some cases this was so, but that an examination might reveal some changes. He knew of one instance in which the testicles of the male were dried up. He did not think this was invariable, however. He had examined Falleni at one time, but just in a general way. She had been brought to him to see if 'it' was a man or a woman. Falleni had consented to be examined, and this had taken half a second, he supposed.

In answer to the judge, Palmer added that as a result of his examination he had found that she was female, but he had not gone beyond that. He had made no internal examination of any sort, he said.

Although this was not evident in the transcript, *Sunday Truth* revealed that McDonnell was now obliged to explain to Sir William Cullen that by these questions he was endeavouring to 'clear up' the matter of 'sex fraud' by showing that there was such a thing as 'true sexual inversion'.

The judge asked, 'Are you setting up insanity, or not?'

'Oh, certainly not,' McDonnell answered. McDonnell continued his questioning, asking Dr Palmer if it was not a fact that when the hands were extended normally in front of the body, palms upward, the elbows of a woman were closer together than the elbows of a man.

Again the judge interjected, apparently with some irritation, saying, 'That might have some bearing on the case if you were setting up insanity, but as you say you are not, I cannot see what this is leading to.'

McDonnell answered, perhaps a little lamely, 'I want to show, Your Honour, that the accused has the masculine angle of arms,' reported *Truth*.

Now McDonnell returned yet again to the question of violence to the body, and during another lengthy interlude covering the same ground, Palmer commented that there was no better way of destroying signs of violence than by fire.

Coyle, in a re-examination of Palmer, returned to the situation of the body at the site of death. Palmer reiterated that he had been taken to the site only to examine the body and decide whether it should be removed to the morgue immediately. He had not concerned himself with the position of the picnic fire and the burnt ground. He had not made notes; the police were there making notes, they had found the bottle and the other evidence. He had only noticed that there was no evidence of a fire having been built around the body.

Coyle then asked whether the seventh crack, if it had been caused by an act of violence, would have rendered the woman unconscious. Palmer thought that it would have, although he could not say how long that unconsciousness might have lasted. It could have been a short while, or two or three days. If burned while unconscious, she would have been incapable of moving. Palmer could not say how far the fire had spread, that had not been his concern.

A conscious woman catching fire would exhibit plenty of movement, he said. She would wake up if she were asleep. She might have rolled down the hill, or writhed in agony. She might have got up and run 'some distance'. 'Unfortunately,' he added, 'they generally run.'

No conclusion as to her consciousness or unconsciousness could be drawn from the position of the body, said Palmer. After running, she might have fallen and then twisted and convulsed. It seemed unlikely, however, that she would have run straight up the hill.

A final series of questions from McDonnell concerned the time of death, as estimated by the quantity of food in the woman's stomach. If the woman had lain unconscious for three or four days before burning, said Palmer, the normal process of digestion would have continued, and he would not in that case have expected to find food in the woman's stomach. The sort of injury that would have halted the process of digestion would probably have resulted in her death.

Dr Palmer retired and was replaced by Dr Stratford Sheldon, who corroborated the previous evidence. He, like Dr Palmer, could not categorically say that heat could not have caused the crack in question, although he also believed it to be the result of violence. Whether it was caused before or after death, he also could not say.

McDonnell's cross-examination of Sheldon touched on the possibility of poisoning, about which Sheldon said he couldn't make a judgement, as little evidence of poisoning would remain after the body was burnt. After the exhumation an analysis had shown traces of copper, but this could possibly be from the coffin fittings—a source of great trouble to the medical profession in these examinations, he added. On re-examination by Coyle, Sheldon reiterated that the only firm conclusion that the two doctors had reached was that the woman was alive when burnt.

JOHN JOSEPH FELIZ MCMANUS, medical doctor of dentistry, practising at Darling Street, Balmain, next gave evidence. He identified a photograph, exhibit B, as being of Mrs Birkett, and said that he had attended her professionally. The details of the lower denture he made for her he had obtained from the loose leaf ledger he kept, he told Coyle. Mrs Birkett had had all her original teeth extracted. She had first come to see him on 5 February 1913, and then again on 18 February: He had made the denture from fourteen teeth known as gum block teeth on 18 October of the same year, and in number, quality and character they corresponded to the teeth now produced in court.

McDonnell, in his cross-examination, seemed to be trying to shake McManus's recognition of the lower teeth, which McManus admitted he could not definitely identify, as he had on occasion supplied similar teeth to other patients. There was some discussion of the techniques of making gold and rubber plates, and of individual marks of workmanship, and after saying that he was not in a position to identify the woman's upper set of dentures at all, McManus was dismissed.

THE next witness was Harry Gordon Vernon, also a dentist, practising in Sydney and living at Beecroft. He had performed dental work for a Mrs Birkett in August 1910, he said. He remembered the name distinctly, but the dates he had had to get from his records. Dr Clarke at Wahroonga, for whom Mrs Birkett had worked, he also knew well. In 1910 he had made an upper and a lower denture for Mrs Birkett, and to the best of his belief the upper denture was the one now before him. There were various small details on the plate that it was his practice to include. During cross-examination by McDonnell, Vernon did not depart from this.

JOHN GRAY, undertaker, of Burren Street, Erskineville, was called next. Gray told Coyle that he had gone to the City Morgue in October 1917 and got a body there, rolled up in canvas, which he and the keeper had put in a coffin. He could not tell what it was, he said. He had taken it to the City Mortuary, where someone took it off his hands.

Gray had gone to the morgue some time this year, he continued. He was asked to identify the coffin, which he did by the name plate.

Under cross-examination by McDonnell, the undertaker said that he handled a good many bodies, including unidentified female ones, and this type of tin plate, marked 'Unknown', and 'adult female' was used to distinguish them. He admitted that this particular nameplate could be from another such body.

Coyle pressed him on this point, and then he was dismissed.

The police photographer, Sergeant Crichton Stevenson, testified that in October 1917 he had taken photographs of the site of the death, which was pointed out to him by Inspector Maze and Detective Ferguson as being where a murder had been committed. He identified the tendered photographs as the ones he had taken, and these were also marked as exhibits.

Thirteen

IN MORE MODERN TIMES, if you drive off the six-lane expressway that is now Epping Road at the Lane Cove River, and head back east along Mowbray Road towards Cumberland Avenue, you discover that much of the surrounding area remains as the same bushland it was in 1917. Lane Cove River Park lies to the north of the river, and Mowbray Park to the south. The river itself narrows somewhat, becoming a stretch of water a stone's throw across, with a littoral of soft mud and mangrove-like vegetation lined with discarded beer bottles and plastic forks. Not far from the expressway the noise of traffic is muted, and the only sound is the crowing of roosters in the distance from the CSIRO Research Station across the water.

The day I drove out there it was hot and sunny, with a stiff breeze coming from the northwest that rustled the leaves of the trees. I parked my car near the women's sportsground and picked my way through the half-buried car tyres to the river's edge. The water was muddy and green and wind-ruffled, the air moist and oppressive.

Birds called intermittently, and an old man with a canvas overnight bag drifted past on one of the tracks.

On the sports field a lone woman ran on the spot, solitary in the vast expanse of green.

Higher on the hill, Mowbray Road leads to red-brick suburban 1930s houses with close-trimmed lawns and oleander bushes, where women in shorts water their roses with sprinkler attachments. There is one Federation-style house that seems to be the earliest of the present dwellings. A neighbour confirms that the hillside used to be a dairy farm, and this the original farmhouse.

Further on, at Mowbray Park, the hillside is steeper and thickly wooded with red and grey gums and outcrops of limestone. Now the parrots grow quite raucous in the thick undergrowth. I walked through spiky grass and ferns to a rocky outcrop a hundred feet above the river, where the wind felt pleasantly cool. There were still wildflowers—white flannel flowers and little spotted purple native lilies—that children might pick, but the country was rough once you left the beaten track.

The area was beautiful, in a harsh way. A welcome change from the stifling confines of the inner suburbs; a peaceful place to go for a picnic on a public holiday. I imagined two figures walking, a tall, thin woman in a long skirt and coat, wearing a wide-brimmed hat and worn but sensible boots, and a stockier male figure in grey coat and pants, carrying a cardboard suitcase.

Fourteen

ON THE FRIDAY before Eight Hour Day, 1917, as she was going from her home at Tambourine Bay at three in the afternoon, maintained Eliel Irene Carrol in her evidence, she saw a man sitting on the point about five minutes walk from the paper mills.

The man had his head in his hands. When she passed within a few feet of him, he was startled, and looked up. Mrs Carrol continued on to the paper mills. Half an hour later, returning, she again saw the man. He was sitting in a different place, and when he heard her approach, he looked up, appearing excited. She had looked for him in his original place, she told the court, because he had been staring at the canal and she had thought he was going to commit suicide. Here Mrs Carrol made some further comments about the man's demeanour, which were objected to by McDonnell and not recorded in the court transcript.

He had jumped over the rock and walked behind her for about six minutes, she continued, and then passed her and disappeared in the direction in which the body was later found.

This part of Mrs Carrol's testimony was an apparent departure from her statement at the Police Court, as reported in the newspapers at that date. Then she had said that she had seen the man on the Sunday afternoon before Eight Hour Day rather than the Friday.

More recently, Mrs Carrol had identified Eugenia Falleni from a police line-up of twenty men as the man she had seen three years before, wearing dark grey trousers, navy blue coat and dark grey hat, near the paper mills. In the line-up, Mrs Carrol testified, Falleni had been wearing almost identical clothes, except for a shirt and stiff collar.

Mr McDonnell, for the defence, tried to shake this evidence by asking Mrs Carrol if she had read about the case in the newspapers before making the identification. Mrs Carrol denied this. She had seen a picture in the paper a week before she made the identification, she said, but had not read the article. Her mother had shown her the paper doubled under, and asked her if she had ever seen the face before. She said yes, but she had not read the story, she repeated. She denied that she had been shown a photograph of Falleni at any other time, or by anyone else.

Mrs Carrol had known the Lane Cove area since she was a child, she said. She was sure of the date on which she had seen the man, she claimed, as she had not been out there for some years. She remembered that a body had been found out there a few days later, but she had not connected the two events till months afterwards.

Detective Walsh had asked her to give evidence at the Police Court, she replied to McDonnell. He told her that it had been reported to him that she had seen a man in the locality at the time the body was found. She did not know how he had come by the information. Mrs Carrol had told a number of people, including some in the area, about having seen the man, but she would not like to mention their names in case they did not want to be drawn into the matter.

Mrs Carrol said she had described the man as having eyes of a grey-hazel colour, neither brown nor grey, and a prominent chin and straight, droopy mouth.

According to the *Sun* of 5 October, there was a tense minute in court when Mr McDonnell, in a further effort to shake this identification, asked the witness to approach the dock and see if the accused's eyes were hazel. Eugenia rose quickly and, gripping the dock front, leaned forward slightly and gazed intently at Mrs Carrol. Her hand trembled as she released her grip on the dock and resumed her seat. After some discussion about the colour of Eugenia's eyes, during which McDonnell pressed her to admit that the eyes were blue, Mrs Carrol said that they were grey. This ended her evidence.

CLARA BONE testified that she and her husband, Ernest Bone, had a grocery shop at the corner of Lyons Road and Gipps Street, Drummoyne, where they had lived for a number of years. She had known the Crawfords for about twenty months from 1915, and during that time Harry Birkett, the son, had worked for her. That was three years ago, she said. She had always known Harry Crawford as a man. In 1916 and 1917 her husband and she had had a cottage at Collaroy beach, and she confirmed that she had taken the boy there for the Eight Hour Day holiday, in 1917, from Saturday afternoon to Monday evening, along with her mother and her family.

Mrs Crawford would come to do domestic duties sometimes, as a favour, when Mrs Bone's maid was on holidays, but she was not then generally working for a living. Mrs Bone had last seen her perhaps a week before Eight Hour Day.

Her husband Ernest Bone had not gone to the beach cottage with them on that occasion. He had seen Harry Crawford the day after Eight Hour Day, Tuesday, when he had come and asked the boy to come home early. She herself had had a conversation with Crawford on Wednesday, around noon, when he had come to pay an account for some groceries. At this time Crawford had said that his wife had gone away with another man. Mrs Bone had told him she did not believe him. He had seemed excited and flurried, she said, and he had taken the boy away with him. She did not see the boy again until perhaps twelve months later, when he came back to see if she had news of his mother. She had also had a letter from him.

On the same Wednesday after Eight Hour Day Mrs Bone had seen Joel Hart's van at Crawford's gate, which she could see from her place. Hart, a furniture remover with a second-hand shop, had been carting away furniture.

Whenever Mrs Crawford had been at her place she had drunk a lot of tea—but nothing else, said Mrs Bone. During 1917 she could say from her own knowledge that Crawford and his wife were very unhappy.

To McDonnell, Mrs Bone described the Crawfords as neighbours and customers. She admitted having told the Police Court that she had seen them walking arm-in-arm on Sunday nights. Although she had concluded from what Mrs Birkett had said to her that they were unhappy, there were times when they appeared happy.

Ernest Bone, Clara's husband, corroborated his wife's account. He had carried on a grocery business at Lyons Road for fifteen years, he said. He had known Harry Crawford, whom he knew as a man, for five years. When Harry Birkett had gone away with his wife for the weekend to Collaroy beach, he had stayed behind at the shop.

He had seen Harry Crawford that same Saturday afternoon, coming down Lyons Road. 'Hello, just getting home?' he asked, and Crawford had answered yes. Crawford had then said to him, 'The bugger has cleared out.'

'Who?' asked Bone.

'The Missus,' answered the other. 'She goes away with other men.'

Bone replied, 'I do not think she is a woman like that.'

Crawford said, 'I can bloody well prove it. I have letters.'

Bone said that Crawford was very excited and smelt of whisky. He was glad to get out of his company, the way he was speaking, he added. He was not at all friendly with Crawford himself.

They had spoken about young Harry being away, and then Crawford went towards his home.

On the following Wednesday, Bone again saw Crawford, but they did not speak. The key to Harry and Annie's home was subsequently left for him to give to Wyatt, the landlord, and he did not encounter Crawford again until he saw him at the Police Court. After a brief cross-examination by McDonnell, Ernest Bone retired.

Eugenia: A Man

AFTER a fifteen-minute adjournment at 4 p.m., Jane Wigg, the former neighbour now residing at Concord, was called. In 1917, she said, she had lived at 'Iris', No. 7 The Avenue in Drummoyne, and Mr and Mrs Crawford had lived in No. 5.

Shown photographs of the houses in The Avenue, Mrs Wigg indicated her own. The Crawfords lived next door, she said: the one with the tree in front. She used to see Mrs Crawford about twice a week, sometimes more.

On the Friday before Eight Hour Day, before lunch, she had seen Mr and Mrs Crawford come out of their gate and walk up The Avenue towards Lyons Road and then turn the corner towards the tram. She had stood on her verandah and watched them, and then had walked out to her own gate. One of them was carrying a small suitcase, and Mrs Crawford was wearing a gabardine raincoat. That was the last she saw of Mrs Crawford, and she did not see Mr Crawford again until the following Wednesday morning, when the furniture was being carried from the house and put in a cart.

McDonnell's first questions to Mrs Wigg concentrated on the Crawfords' relationship. Mrs Wigg did not observe their conduct, she said, but thought they got on very well.

McDonnell touched on the matter of the suitcase and its description, and queried her on what she had read in the newspapers or heard about the case prior to being questioned by the detectives. Mrs Wigg could not remember, but thought that Detective Watkins might have said something about 'the man-woman'. She had given a written statement and signed it. She felt perfectly certain that the last time she had seen Mrs Crawford had been that Friday, in the afternoon, and had given her reasons for fixing on that date.

JOEL HART, retired second-hand dealer of 25 Renwick Street, Drummoyne, gave evidence that he had bought some furniture from a man named Crawford who worked at Perdriau's rubber works. He bought the furniture on Wednesday 3 October 1917, after being requested to look at it a day or two before. Crawford had said that he wanted £10 for the furniture and he had agreed.

On the Wednesday, Crawford had seemed excited, and Hart said he could not help asking if there was a bill of sale over the goods, or a time payment. He wanted the information for his own protection, he told Coyle. Crawford had said no, and asked what made him ask that.

Hart said he usually saw the wife when he bought furniture from a man, because he did not like breaking up a house for nothing. Crawford had told him that his wife was over at North Sydney, and that was all he could remember. There were also sundry boxes of crockery and other things that Hart took to someone else to be minded. He delivered those, and then removed the furniture he had bought himself. He thought the name of the people to whom he took the boxes was Parnell.

THE NEXT witness was Emma Belbin, married woman, living at Waverley. She had been living in Balmain in 1917, she said, and was a friend of the Parnell family, whom she used to visit in Cometrowe Street,

Drummoyne. She had first encountered the accused early in October 1917, at Mrs Parnell's house. He was dressed in working clothes and wearing a blue gabardine shirt, and was introduced to her as Mr Crawford. She had thought he was ill. It was the Tuesday night after Eight Hour Day, which had been the Monday. Crawford was sitting by the fire with his head in his hands, and she had had no conversation with him.

Subsequently she had seen him again at the Parnells' house, but again they did not speak. After that she saw him frequently, and he told her that his wife had left him. She drank, and he would not have her back again, he said.

Mrs Belbin had seen Crawford himself drink ale and beer, she told Coyle.

In answer to McDonnell, Mrs Belbin admitted that she had seen the accused drunk on more than one occasion. This was mostly at parties, some of which were at her house, to which Mrs Parnell had brought him at Mrs Belbin's invitation. They were not beer parties, although beer and tea were served, and they would break up around midnight. She had also seen Crawford under the influence of liquor on the street.

Twice she had written a letter for Crawford. As far as she knew, he could not read and write.

JABEZ JAMES HICKS, an orchardist of Ryde, who in 1917 was employed at the Cumberland Paper Mills, identified Falleni as the man he had seen at the canal near the mills on Sunday 30 September 1917, between 5.30 and 7.30 in the morning. He had noticed something peculiar about the walk—short quick steps, he said—and the pronounced swing of the right arm of the man. This, he claimed, had allowed him to identify the accused in a line-up of fifteen to twenty men at the Police Court three years later.

In answer to McDonnell, Hicks said that he had not known there was a woman in male attire among their number. He denied that the photograph published in the *Sun* had enabled him to identify the man, although he had seen it, he admitted.

JAMES WOODBURY, of Gore Hill, also identified the accused as the person he had seen near the mills on 30 September. He worked as a watchman, he told Mr Coyle, and on other days as a labourer at the paper mills. He had been so close to the man he could have touched him, he said: he seemed 'peculiar' in manner, and had looked in the direction in which the body was later found. He had then continued on towards the flour mills, and Woodbury had lost sight of him.

In answer to McDonnell, Woodbury testified that at that particular time he was employed as an extra watchman on the weekend shift, and had taken the morning watch from five in the morning to one in the afternoon. He had seen the man at about 7.00 a.m., an unusual time for anyone to pass by there. He had not mentioned the man when the police had first come making inquiries about the body found there, he said, because he did not want to be drawn into anything.

At 5.30 p.m. on 5 October 1920, with the prosecutor still having eleven witnesses to call, Sir William Cullen adjourned the court until ten the following morning. The jury were locked up for the night and not permitted contact with the public. Eugenia spent the night at the Central Police Station in the cells.

Fifteen

AMONG 27 streets called 'The Avenue' in my modern edition of *Gregory's Street Directory*, none was listed for Drummoyne. I went back to the Reading Room. In the Premier street directory for 1934, the earliest the Mitchell Library could supply, the index listed a total of eight streets called 'The Avenue'. Two were in the general area of Drummoyne, in Hunter's Hill and Balmain, but none was in Drummoyne itself.

Mystified, and about to put the tattered volume back, I glanced at the map covering Drummoyne, and the first thing that caught my eye, north of Lyons Road and running down towards Five Dock Bay parallel to Moore Street, was an unlisted 'The Avenue'. Now it had become a continuation of Gipps Street, although in 1934 the old name had survived on the map, if not in the index. Nos. 5 and 7 The Avenue, (now most likely 87 and 89 Gipps Street), where Harry and Annie had first moved from Kogarah, reveal themselves today as small wooden workers' cottages with tiny front gardens, about a mile and a half from the Chiswick ferry wharf.[5]

---

5   My thanks to Mark Tedeschi for discovering an error in my original identification of this address. See Tedeschi, Mark, *Eugenia* (2012) Note 6 to Chapter Four, page 252.

No. 87, where Harry had sat at the kitchen table drinking whisky after the Labour Day weekend of 1917, was well-tended and half-hidden from the wide street by a wall of trees and shrubs. Probably in 1917 the street was a little less sheltered on a hot day, a little less neatly groomed, when Annie and Harry walked up to Lyons Road to do their shopping.

Next I went to Cathedral Street, which in 1917 was a straight road running down from the green lawns and shady trees of Hyde Park, past the steps of the imposing St Mary's Cathedral, and into the heart of Woolloomooloo. Then, with its upper reaches crowded with cheap boarding houses for foreign sailors and single men, its lower areas were the territory of a formidable local push, or gang of larrikins, and the rough pubs near the wharves provided a sanctuary for some of the toughest prostitutes in Sydney.

Today, Woolloomooloo still survives as an old, inner-city residential suburb caught somewhere between preservation, gentrification and development. I was quite surprised to find that 103 Cathedral Street, where Mrs Schieblich had let a room to Harry Crawford and his stepson, was still standing. On the opposite side of the road a row of handsome Victorian terraces had been expensively converted to pristine, glass-fronted shops.

But 103 Cathedral Street, a dilapidated liver-brick building with an austere, geometrical front, battles on. Squat, solid, three storeys high and running the entire length of its site, it boasts a cocky brick false façade designed to give it a more impressive height. Wrought iron bars guard its windows, a blue plastic awning perches above its olive-green front door like a gambler's eyeshade on a rather imposing old spinster. When I first went to look at it, its padlocked wooden mailboxes revealed that behind the door—which showed signs that someone had once tried to jemmy it open—were sixteen of what could only be tiny flats. I rather liked the old place. It was not going to give up in a hurry.

I did not ring any of the bells, back then. Only two of the mail boxes displayed names, and one of these was in Japanese. I could not quite see myself trying to explain to a suspicious tenant why I wanted to see inside. I walked down the street, wondering which of the cane-blinded front windows concealed the room that Harry Crawford had told his German landlady was haunted.

156 Cathedral Street, where Mrs Bombelli had lived, no longer existed.

Sixteen

WHEN THE COURT reconvened on Wednesday 6 October, the second day of the trial, the customary crowd had gathered in the courthouse grounds. They were formed into queues, and rushed for seats in the public galleries as soon as the doors were opened. The *Daily Telegraph* commented once more on the remarkable interest shown in the trial by women.

At this point, I thought, there were questions I should ask myself as well. Was I just showing the same morbid curiosity as the women who had crowded into the Darlinghurst courtroom in 1920, craning to see the diminutive figure screened from them in the dock? What was it that they hoped to get from Eugenia?

At worst, they might have been motivated by the same lust for sensation that once drew crowds to public executions. At best, it might have been a fascination with a woman who had stepped outside the suffocating bounds of conventional femininity; who had, literally, run away to sea. No doubt a proportion of these female spectators condemned Eugenia, and wanted to see her punished for breaking the rules that they themselves abided by; but would there not have been many who were secretly exhilarated by her grasping the freedom to go where she wished, work where she wished, live as she wished and remain unharassed for doing so? No matter how illusory this freedom had proved to be?

It was a chilling picture that the prosecution was painting for the twelve male jurors: emerging was a woman who was a liar, probably an alcoholic, violent-tempered and abusive, and perhaps capable of committing a murder for little other reason than convenience. The public was no doubt already satisfied from the newspapers that she was a sexual freak and an unsuccessful child killer. What was it in me, I wondered, that despite all this, wanted against all the circumstantial evidence for Eugenia to be innocent? And why, for all her honesty, naiveté and decency, was it so hard to feel any substantial sympathy for the unfortunate Annie Birkett?

THE PROSECUTION'S first witness on the second day was Marcellina Bombelli, of 156 Cathedral Street, Sydney. Signora Bombelli gave evidence with the help of an interpreter, Dr Charles Albert Monticone. She had known the accused as 'Nina' for about ten years, Mrs Bombelli told Coyle. She had been told that the accused was a woman, but had never seen her dressed as one.

Nina had brought Harry Birkett to her house in November 1917, and asked her to take in the boy. His father was dead and his mother ill in hospital with consumption, Nina told her. Signora Bombelli had never received any payment, but Nina had brought her some linen and cutlery, saying she had no use for them. The two of them spoke only in Italian, although little was said.

Mrs Bombelli kept the boy for about a year. She identified some linen and cutlery produced in court as that given to her by Nina.

SIGNORA BOMBELLI was followed by Lydia Parnell, who gave evidence similar to that she had given at the Central Police Court. Mrs Parnell was again distressed, and spoke with difficulty at times. Living in the same neighbourhood, she said, she had often discussed domestic troubles with Harry Crawford, whom she knew as a man. Harry had told her he could not get on with his wife, and that she was dissatisfied with him. He also told her that his wife had threatened to run away with another man. Over a period of weeks, whenever there was a quarrel he would come and tell her about it. However, when she saw the couple together, they seemed to outward appearances affectionate. She would see them out shopping together on Saturday mornings, arm-in-arm.

On Eight Hour Day, Monday, 1917, she had seen Harry Crawford coming from the tram terminus between 7.15 and 7.45 in the evening, but had avoided him because she was on her way to the pictures and did not want to be delayed.

She saw him again next morning, when he came to her house and asked if she could give him some breakfast. He had seemed upset, and told her that his wife had not been home all night. Later she gave the boy breakfast also. She saw Crawford two or three times that day, and the conversation was always about his wife not having come home.

Crawford had asked if Mrs Parnell's son George could go around and help the carter move furniture.

Eugenia: A Man

She later went to the house to find her son and saw the furniture being removed. She thought it was the same day she had given them breakfast, but it might not have been. It was a long time ago now, she said.

There had also been the matter of a diamond ring. On the Saturday prior to Eight Hour Day Crawford had come to her house in the afternoon and asked if she would mind two rings, as his wife had threatened to run away with a plumber, he said. He told Mrs Parnell the rings were his property, as he had bought them for his wife, and he would not allow her the benefit of taking them away. Mrs Parnell minded the rings for some weeks. Some boxes and a carryall were also left at her house and she understood these contained household linen. Three days later Crawford returned with a carter and took them away.

Until March 1918, when Mrs Parnell had left Drummoyne for Newcastle, Harry Crawford had continued to visit the house frequently. He was just like one of their own, she said. He always spoke of his wife and seemed anxious to find her. She did not see Harry Birkett again.

Up until Christmas in 1917 Mrs Parnell often had conversations with Crawford about his wife, and he would tell her that he went to certain places he thought she might visit. In the meantime he went to work in Manly. Then one day near Christmas 1917 he told Mrs Parnell that he had bumped into his wife in George Street, outside the Palais de Danse, and she had asked him for money. He did not have any to give her, and had jumped on the tram and left her there, he said.

In the course of a brief cross-examination by

McDonnell, Mrs Parnell testified that Harry Crawford had not said when his wife had left, but she had taken it that she had gone the day before. She did not ask, she said. Crawford had told her that he was breaking up his home because Mrs Crawford had previously done the same thing to him in Balmain. Mrs Crawford had left his boxes on the edge of the pavement, he said, and he would do the same to her.

Mrs Parnell said she was not on friendly terms with Mrs Crawford, but she was with Harry Crawford. She had simply come to the conclusion that Mrs Crawford had gone off somewhere after a husband-and-wife quarrel, and would probably return.

GEORGE WILLIAM PARNELL, clerk, who lived at present with his mother in Newcastle, also gave evidence that he knew Harry Crawford. He corroborated his mother's description of Crawford's having come to their house one morning just after Eight Hour Day—it might have been the Wednesday—and asking him to help move furniture, which he did. He had helped get it ready to put on the cart. Crawford had abused his wife for having left him—he called her a 'bloody bastard', if he remembered rightly.

Crawford had asked him to look at a newspaper to see if any bodies had been found, or if any suicides had occurred. George Parnell read to him a report of the discovery of a charred body at Chatswood, and Crawford had exclaimed, 'That's the bugger, that's her!' At the time Crawford was working in the Hotel Steyne in Manly. He also recalled Crawford telling his mother that he had seen his wife near the Palais de Danse.

McDonnell, for the defence, asked Parnell if Crawford had previously ever asked him to read from a newspaper.

Parnell replied that he had looked in the 'wanted' column for a position for him; that was all. He believed that Crawford could not read.

He knew of the discovery of the body only from what he had read in the paper, he told McDonnell, and it had not crossed his mind that it was his duty to report Crawford's remark to anyone in authority. He told his mother what Crawford had said, but otherwise he was not interested, and had not asked any questions.

MRS EDITH HOYES, another neighbour in Drummoyne, had been living at No. 3 The Avenue, for eight years, she told Coyle. She had known Crawford since January 1917, when the couple had come next door to live. Harry Crawford had returned home between seven and eight on the Monday evening after Eight Hour Day. She had had a conversation with him at the gate, during which he had told her that his wife had gone away.

'Where to?' she had asked.

'I don't know,' he said. Looking agitated, he told her that his wife had left him with nothing. The next time Mrs Hoyes saw the accused was when he came to her house a couple of months later. He had asked if she had heard or seen anything of Mrs Crawford, or if anyone had been inquiring about her. She could not remember his exact words, but he had seemed relieved that she had not, and then became quite talkative.

She had often seen Mrs Crawford coming and going when the couple had lived next door, and she had always seemed a very quiet, ladylike and refined woman. And no, she had never seen her under the influence of liquor.

In reply to Mr McDonnell, Mrs Hoyes said that Falleni, while masquerading as a man, had always appeared decent and respectable. She, also, had seen Harry Crawford and Annie walking arm-in-arm. She had not heard him use coarse and vulgar language.

Mrs Hoyes could not say when she had last seen Mrs Crawford, but it must have been during the week before Eight Hour Day. She had not asked Crawford questions about when his wife had disappeared. There had not been a lot of gossip among the neighbours, although it was not usual for one of a married couple to disappear like that. She did not trouble herself much with the neighbours, she finished.

DR STRATFORD SHELDON, recalled, gave evidence in response to McDonnell that he had been informed that he had examined Harry Crawford on one occasion for a claim under the *Workers' Compensation Act*, although he had no recollection of it himself. He had once known the accused, he said, but that was eight years ago, and now he would not have recognised her on the street. He could check the occasion in his files, but his only present knowledge of it was because someone had told him of it. He was prepared to accept the fact that she had come to his rooms.

With reference to Falleni's mode of walking, Dr Sheldon stated that he did not consider that the injury to the arm due to the little finger being pulled out by machinery would be sufficient to alter the carriage of the arm or the balance.

At McDonnell's request (according to the *Sun* newspaper):

> Dr Sheldon approached the dock and the accused extended her right hand over the front. The little finger was missing. The doctor pulled the sleeve up, felt the muscles of the well shaped arm, got the accused to flex her fingers and arm, and then declared that there was no evidence of contraction of the ligatures.

The suggestion that the tendons had been torn out was not apparent in the muscle movement of the arm, the doctor reported. Then he was dismissed.

ANOTHER witness, George Robert Smith, of Elswick Street in Leichhardt, who in 1917 had lived in Bush Street, Drummoyne, testified that he had been to Crawford's house on a Friday night to inquire if Mrs Crawford could come and do some housework as his wife was ill. Crawford had left Drummoyne the week after, he remembered. Crawford had told him that his wife had 'cleared out with a plumber', and on going inside he had seen that everything was packed up ready to go. He had agreed to look after a sewing machine, a trunk and a hat box, which he had kept over the weekend. He could not remember whether the Friday in question was before Eight Hour Day or after, but he was sure it was a Friday. He had not seen Mrs Crawford on that occasion.

Mrs Crawford was a tall, thin, refined woman who kept to herself, he said. The Crawfords had seemed an ill-assorted pair: one day they would be getting on all right and the next day rowing. There seemed to be an irritation between them, Smith observed, at some times more decided than others.

HENRIETTA SCHIEBLICH, who from the *Sunday Truth* sketch was a handsome woman in a large feathered or veiled hat with the brim turned up off her face, had been living at 103 Cathedral Street, Woolloomooloo, for six years, she said. Speaking with a distinct accent, and in ungrammatical English, she told Coyle that she had first seen the accused (whom she referred to as Mrs Falleni), the third day after she first saw something in the paper about a murder at Chatswood. He had given his name as Jack Crawford and had taken a front room in her house with two single beds for himself and his stepson.

Crawford arrived two days after that with Harry Birkett and a good many trunks and boxes. He had seemed very excited and smoked heavily. Two days later he saw in a newspaper a photograph of a pair of shoes, and called Harry Birkett into a room to read it to him. Crawford then told Henrietta Schieblich that if 'two big men' called they would be detectives, and she should not tell them that he was there. Crawford also broke up two big boxes with an axe, telling Mrs Schieblich that his wife had left him. When she asked if his wife might not return, he said something like, 'No, no, I want her no more, she is no good, no good, no good, drinking too much.'

Later he told her, 'I had a jolly good row with her, and gave her a jolly good crack on the head to go on with.' When Mrs Schieblich said that he should not hit a woman so hard, it was not nice, he had seemed 'very sad', and sat on her table with his head in his hands.

When the boxes were broken up, Mrs Schieblich noticed that they had contained some beautiful linen and lace and curtains. After some time the question of payment came up, and Crawford gave her some clothes—ladies' garments—in lieu of payment, as well as thirty shillings. Mrs Schieblich identified these clothes in court. She had accepted them although they were too small for her, she told Coyle.

Crawford had also burnt some papers and lace in the fire under the copper in her absence, and later she found a pair of scissors. There was no one else living in the house at the time who had these sorts of things. There were only gentlemen, she told Coyle, although later there was a girl.

Soon after, the boy went away to the Italian people, said Mrs Schieblich. Crawford had stayed on in the same room by himself. It was a few days after the boy had left that Crawford had come downstairs and said to her, 'Madame, Madame, the room is haunted, I am haunted.'

Later, after she had falsely told him that two detectives had been making inquiries, Jack Crawford had left. By that time he had been at her house a month or two. A couple of weeks later he had visited her again, saying he had been living with his wife at North Sydney, but then had left her again on account of her drinking habits.

In answer to McDonnell, Mrs Schieblich said that she adhered to her description that Crawford had sometimes acted as if he were partly mad. He was often very excited, she added.

Mrs Schieblich described in detail an arrangement she had made with Crawford that he should pay five shillings a week per bed, and how after a few weeks he and the boy took full board at fifteen shillings each. She denied that the apparel and linen she had been given to make up payment had been a present.

Crawford said his wife had screamed very loud when he hit her, at the time they had had the row and she left, she told McDonnell. Mrs Schieblich had asked, 'For what you hit her so hard?' Crawford had also said that Harry Birkett was away on a picnic at the time.

She had not questioned Crawford further about the blow, but she did say on one occasion, 'I think you killed her,' on account of his excited demeanour, his crying and laughing. She had not really meant it, but she could not help saying it. She had thought that something was 'funny' on account of the way he acted.

She had not gone to the police, she told McDonnell, because she was a German, and her husband and son at that time had been in an internment camp for five years and she felt she could not do it. She had to go every week to report to the Police Station at the Military barracks. She had never had anything to do with the police in Germany, she said, but she did not report these things to the police because of the fact that she was German.

In response to further questions from McDonnell concerning some variations in her statements, Mrs Schieblich denied that she often told lies, despite her falsely telling Crawford, to get rid of him, that detectives had been looking for him. She was telling the truth today, she maintained. She denied that she told the truth only when it suited her. She had not been sure Crawford was a criminal, she had merely had suspicions.

After Crawford left her house, he had stayed away for a good while, Mrs Schieblich continued. She was not sure when he had first come back. First he came back from the North Shore and stayed a little while, and then he went to Balmain to a meat factory, and it was after this that his little finger had been cut off.

Mrs Schieblich had had a minor dispute with her lodger. Just before Jack Crawford had left for the first time, for the North Shore, he had said to her, referring to her husband, 'Don't live with this bloody German any more.' A young gentleman and a girl at the house had left at the same time. The girl told Mrs Schieblich that Jack Crawford had told them to leave and to have no more to do with 'a bloody German'. Mrs Schieblich denied to McDonnell that this had annoyed her; she had taken very little notice, she said. She had had no fixed resentment against Jack Crawford.

At the time, however, 'I was heartbroken myself,' she told the court. 'I was in very bad circumstances.' Jack Crawford did not stay long after coming back from the North Shore, only a couple of weeks. But he came back four times in all. Added together, those times would amount to about two years, Mrs Schieblich thought. When he came back from Balmain, he did not have very much money, but he paid her ten shillings a week and she was satisfied.

ALICE MAUD GOUGH, married woman, gave evidence that she had known the accused for about a month when she had lived at 61 Morton Street,

Rozelle, in 1918. He had boarded at No. 59, next door, and she had known him as Harry Crawford, she told Mr Coyle. They had had frequent conversations, and he had told her that his wife had left him and gone away with another man. He had a daughter, he said, and his wife had a son; she was married before and so was he. He told her that his wife was a drunkard, and that when he came back from work the crockery would be all broken up and no meal ready.

Alice Gough had said to him, 'I cannot understand a woman going away and leaving a man and leaving all her clothes behind. Why did she do that?'

Crawford had answered that his money had paid for everything, and his wife would not take what his money had paid for.

Under cross-examination from McDonnell, Mrs Gough said that, while living next door to her, Crawford had worked in different places, never staying in one place for long. He told her he had got a position in a hotel on the corner of Market and George Streets, and had left because they wanted him to get outside and clean the windows and he did not want to fall and break his neck. She would see him before he went to work, and they would hold a conversation over the back fence. At other times she would see him walking along the street. He was always a mystery to her, she said. She had noticed something about his carriage, his walk—he had a swinging walk, a nervous sort of walk, which she could not explain properly. He always swung both arms. He put her in mind of a man on stilts, or something of that sort. He swung both arms equally. He told her he was looking for a job in the meatworks, but things were bad and he would have to wait. He was not missing a finger then, she maintained, when he lived next door to her.

FRANK BOMBELLI, called next, said he was a foreman of a motor body works at Waterloo, and lived at Stanmore. He knew the accused as Crawford, he told Coyle, but not by any Christian name. He saw the accused some years ago, down in Rose Bay. In 1917 he had brought Harry Birkett to his mother's place, he said. He had bought a pawn ticket for a diamond ring from Crawford, for which he paid one pound. This he kept, and after some time redeemed.

Frank Bombelli identified Exhibit M, a diamond ring, as that diamond ring, which he had later given to Detective Robson, he said.

JOHN HENRY WALSH, a police constable stationed at North Sydney in 1917, described to Coyle the events of 2 October of that year. In consequence of a message received, he said, he had gone with Inspector Moss to the Cumberland Paper Mills and talked to a boy named Howard. Then they went together to a rough, rocky and timbered area a short distance to the north of the paper mills, towards Mowbray Road, where he had found the burnt body of a dead female, lying on her back facing east. Underneath the body was a small piece of gabardine. In the area were found various other objects, already produced in court, which he identified: a pair of stockings, a pair of shoes, a full set of false upper teeth and some lower teeth, a broken quart flagon with the name 'Robert' blown in the glass, a kidney-shaped piece of greenstone, a glass and an enamel mug (found alongside the bottle), the corner pieces and lock of what appeared to be a carryall or a hamper, a small knife, and a hat pin. According to the *Sun* newspaper, Falleni watched the shifting of these things from place to place with great attention, moving occasionally in the dock, although she remained composed.

Behind the body was a rock about nine feet high, said Walsh. On the left hand side of the body the flames had spread for some distance, and had been high enough to reach the top of a nearby tree. The body was on the outskirts of the burnt area, and there seemed to be no traces of a fire constructed around it.

Constable Walsh had first seen the accused on the morning of 22 July 1920 at the Central Police Station, where she was lined up, dressed in male clothing, with a number of other men. He was present when Jabez James Hicks identified her as the person he'd seen at Lane Cove between 5.30 and 7.00 a.m. on 28 September 1917.

At 2.30 p.m. on the same day, 22 July 1920, together with Detective Leary, Detective Sergeant Robson, Hicks and the accused, he had gone to the scene where the body was found. They went a little distance to the west and Hicks pointed out the spot where he had seen the accused. When Detective Robson asked, 'Do you know this locality?' the accused had answered, 'I have never been here in my life.'

They walked to a rock overlooking the Chicago Flour Mills, and Walsh asked, 'What is that place there?'

'That is where they make cornflour,' the accused replied.

'Well, you do know something about the locality,' said

Eugenia: A Man

Walsh. 'How long did you work in the flour mills?'

The accused answered, 'One week, I could not stand the smell and I left.'

Walsh then said, 'Will you tell me where you lived when you worked at the flour mill?' and the accused answered, 'At Balmain.'

'Will you explain to me how and on what side of the river you came to work of a morning?' asked Walsh.

'I lived with some German people on the other side of the bridge from the mill.'

'Can you tell me their names?'

To which the accused replied, 'I decline to answer any further,' said Walsh.

Walsh described to Coyle how a person might reach the Cumberland Paper Mills from Drummoyne. From The Avenue, he said, one would walk or take a bus to the top of Lyons Road, where the Gladesville tram from Sydney passed. After travelling about a mile by tram to a point just near the Gladesville mental asylum, one would alight to walk to Fig Tree Bridge, another mile away. Some two miles further up Burns Bay Road, which led from the North Shore to Hunters Hill and Gladesville, one would branch off at Charlo's Dairy, and walk down Collins Street (now Cullen Street) to the main road that led to the mills, a distance of another half a mile.

Walsh explained to McDonnell that the Cumberland Paper Mill and the Chicago Flour Mill were about 400 yards apart—'as the crow would fly'. To get from one to the other, one would have to cross the canal at the paper mills, and walk over some very rough country. The ground was sandy and rocky, without much litter, and vegetated with light timber, ti-tree and general scrub. A fallen tree—here the witness demonstrated the position of the rock and the body with a bible and pen—was close to the body.

The body was intact, burnt quickly, said Walsh, but the features were unrecognisable. The fire appeared more severe around the body than around the head. There was a [picnic] fire to the left of the body, but it did not seem to have anything to do with the burning of it. It was included, like the suitcase, in the radius of the fire as it had swept around. The suitcase had no steel frame, and the metal corners and locks had fallen from it as it burnt.

At this point in Walsh's description, the court adjourned for lunch.

At 2.00 p.m., McDonnell concluded his cross-examination of Constable Walsh with some detailed questions concerning the hat wires found, the distance of the body from the paper mills, and the wind direction, from which no new information emerged.

By 2.15 p.m. the journalist from the *Sun* must have been getting bored, because he noted in his account that a Willy Wagtail came to one of the windows at the top of the court, whistled its lively call—'sweet, pretty creature'—and then flew away.

Seventeen

DETECTIVE SERGEANT Stewart Robson, the officer who had been in charge of the investigation—from the newspaper photograph a rather ponderous, heavyset man—was obviously no stranger to the witness box. A fastidious notetaker, in his lengthy and somewhat jargon-ridden testimony he recreated the events surrounding Eugenia's arrest in pedantic detail. Eugenia, it would appear, had remained calm through the terrible moment of discovery, and Robson himself seemed oblivious of its overtones of farce. If Robson's testimony is to be taken at face value, he— and thus presumably also Harry Birkett—apparently remained unaware of Eugenia's true sex until the time of her questioning, during the course of which he also interviewed Lily Nugent, who knew, but appears to have chosen not to share her knowledge with either her nephew or the police.

Early in 1920, began Robson, he had interviewed Harry Birkett. As a result of his conversation with him, at about 11.30 a.m. on 5 July, he had gone with Detective Watkins to the Empire Hotel on the corner of Parramatta Road and Johnston Street, Annandale. In the hotel licensee's office he had interviewed the accused and asked him his name, which the accused gave as Harry Crawford.

'How long have you been working here?' the detective asked him.

'A few weeks,' Crawford replied.

'What nationality are you?'

'What do you want to know that for?' asked Crawford.

'I believe you are Italian,' Robson told him, to which Crawford answered, 'No, I am a Scotsman from Edinburgh.'

Then, Robson testified, he had told the accused that he was going to take him to the Detectives' Office to make further investigations. In Superintendent Bannan's room at the Criminal Investigation Branch at Central Police Station, Sydney, said Robson, Mr Bannan asked if Crawford was willing to make a voluntary statement.[6] Crawford agreed to do so. He went into another room with the official typist, Mr Walker, and made a statement in answer to Robson's questions. After appearing to read it over, Crawford signed it.

This document was now produced in court and read to the jury. Although not included in the transcript, part of it was reprinted in the newspapers during the committal proceedings, as follows:

---

6   Mark Tedeschi has pointed out that Robson in extracting this evidence, had (as was common practice at the time) neither arrested Crawford and taken him before a magistrate, nor fully cautioned and advised him of his right to silence. Neither did his defence counsel challenge this evidence as inadmissible at the time of Falleni's trial. (Tedeschi, Mark, *Eugenia*, Simon and Schuster, Sydney 2012 pp. 170–1).

Eugenia: A Man

My correct name is Harry Crawford, and I
am 44 years of age. I am a Scotchman and
was born at Edinburgh on July 25, 1875.
My father's name was Harry Crawford and
he was a dealer by occupation. My mother's
name was Lizzie Crawford. About eighteen months after I was born I was taken to
New Zealand by my parents and lived first
at Torrie Street, Wellington with them. I
left my parents' home at Torrie Street, Wellington, when about eighteen years of age,
and worked my passage on a vessel—I think
it was the steamship *Australia*—direct to
New South Wales and landed at Sydney.

My first occupation was the 'useful' in the
King's Head Hotel, at the corner of Elizabeth
and Park Streets, Sydney, where I remained for
about six months. From there I went as a useful to an hotel opposite the police station at
Temora, where I stayed only about a fortnight.
I returned to Sydney, and was employed at
a boarding house near St Patrick's Church,
Church Hill, Sydney, kept, I think, by a Mrs
Thotman, for about three months. Since then
up till about 1913 I was employed at various hotels and boarding houses as a useful.

About 1913, while living at No. 1 Sir John
Young's Crescent, I obtained employment
at the National Meatworks, Balmain, and
went to live with Mrs Elliot, Darling Street,
Balmain. I was at the meatworks for about

three years as a general hand. I then went to Barnes' Meatworks, at White Bay, and worked there for about twelve months. I can't say exactly how long. From Barnes' Meatworks I went to work at Perdriau's Factory, where I remained until I was put off, owing to a shortage caused by the great strike of 1917.

I was then living at No. 7 Lyons Road, Drummoyne. I then returned to the National Meatworks at Balmain, and was later on at their branch at Lilyfield. At this time I lived at Mrs Elliot's, Darling Street, Balmain. I then went to Crawford's Hotel, Drummoyne, where I lived on the premises. From there I went to the Coogee Bay Hotel, where I remained, I think, about three months. I then went to live for one week at Mrs Mcintosh's, Flinders Street, opposite a hotel. From there I went to the Railway Hotel [Richardson's], where I remained for about three months. I was then living at Quigley's, Bourke Street, Sydney, near the Women's Hospital, and from there I went to work at the Empire Hotel, Johnston Street and Parramatta Road, Annandale, where I am at present.

I now reside at 47 Durham Street, Stanmore, with my wife, whose maiden name was Lizzie Allison. I was married at the Canterbury Registry Office in September, 1919. Up to that time I was a single man. My wife is the only personal friend I have had since arriving in Australia, either male or female.

After this, said Robson, he left the room for five or ten minutes, then returned and told Crawford he had reason to doubt his statement. He had interviewed Harry Birkett, he said, and also his uncle and aunt, and he believed that Crawford had married Harry Birkett's mother a few years before.

Crawford was going to be confronted with Harry Birkett, Robson told him, but if he wished he could be lined up with other people for identification.

'I don't want to be lined up with a lot of other people. I have enough worry on my head at present,' Crawford replied.

Robson asked if he had any marks on his body that might assist in proving his identity, and Crawford answered no.

'Strip off a little and let us have a look,' Robson suggested, apparently disingenuously.

'No, I object to that,' said Crawford.

Crawford agreed to go before Dr Palmer, the Government Medical Officer. However, in Palmer's presence, after some hesitation, Crawford again refused to be examined.

'I suppose now I will have to go to gaol,' he remarked, on returning to the detective's office. Robson said he was not sure about that.

'What do they do with you when they take you to gaol?' Crawford asked.

'I'm not familiar with their methods, but I believe they give you a good bath and a change of clothes,' Robson told him.

'Can I go in the women's ward?'

'Oh, not quite,' said Robson. 'No chance of that.'

At this point, Robson told the court, Crawford

took him aside. 'Come here,' he said, 'I want to tell you something.' Out of the hearing of the typist, he whispered, 'I want to tell you that I am a woman, not a man.'

When Robson said that this was a matter for the doctor, not for him, to decide, Crawford asked if the doctor was still in his room. On being told yes, he said, 'Well, I think I'd better see him.'

Robson was present when the accused partly disrobed, he testified, and heard Crawford say to the doctor that he was a woman.

'This is a terrible thing. It has been the worry of my life,' Crawford said when they returned from the examination.

When told they would go out to where he was living with his wife and make a search, Robson testified, Crawford said, 'I do not want you to let her know anything.'

'What, do you mean to say that she has not found out anything since you have been living with her?' asked Robson.

'No, she does not know anything,' Crawford answered.

At this juncture, Robson told the court, Harry Birkett appeared and identified the accused as Harry Crawford, who had married his mother a few years before. When Birkett had left the room, Robson read Birkett's statement to the accused.

This document was also produced in court.

After reading it to him, said Robson, he had asked the accused why he had not mentioned this first wife.

'Oh, you have it all now,' said Crawford. 'You have as much as I could tell you. I did not want to say anything about it, she had been drinking a great deal, a source of worry to me, and she had been going with other men.'

'When was the last time you saw your wife?' asked Robson.

'On Friday before Eight Hour Day.'

'In what year?'

'1917,' Crawford answered. 'She sold up the furniture and cleared out.'

'Have you seen her since?' asked Robson.

'Yes, when she came back on the Wednesday.'

'Who did she sell the furniture to?'

'Someone on Lyons Road.'

'What was the last time you actually saw your wife?'

'On the Wednesday night when she came back to get half the money for the furniture.'

'But you just told me she sold the furniture,' said Robson.

'No, that is wrong. It was I that sold the furniture and she came back for half the money.'

'Was that on the Wednesday night immediately after Eight Hour Day?'

'Yes.'

After this exchange, said Robson, he went with Detective Truscott and the accused to 47 Durham Street, Stanmore, and searched the room the accused occupied with his wife—the second wife. The wife was there crying, and the accused said to Robson, 'Let me open the bag and I will give you something that is in it.'

'No, I could not let you do that,' Robson answered.

'Well, don't let her see it.'

'What is in the bag?' Robson asked.

'You will find it, something that I have been using.'

'What is it? Something artificial?'

'Yes, don't let her see it,' Crawford repeated.

'Do you mean that she does not know anything about this?' Robson asked him again.

'No, and I don't want you to let her know,' said Crawford.

'Did your first wife know you were using something like this?'

'No, not till the latter part of our married life. I think someone had been talking,' replied Crawford.

Robson opened a portmanteau and in it he found a loaded revolver and also, he said, 'an exhibit'.

The revolver was produced in court and Robson identified it.

With reference to the other exhibit, continued Robson, he had asked the accused, 'Is this what you referred to as having used on your wife?'

Here the judge interrupted, and Robson explained that by 'exhibit', he meant 'article'.

The accused had replied yes.

The article, not described in the transcript, but apparently an artificial phallus, was tendered in court and marked Exhibit G1.

Detective Sergeant Robson then took the accused to the Central Police Station where she was charged, and she made no answer. Robson was present on 22 July when Mr Hicks identified her in a line-up of men at the Central Police Station. From there, they went to the Lane Cove River in company with Hicks and Constable Walsh. On the 29th of that month, Mrs Carrol had identified the accused in a police line-up as the person she had seen in that locality, Robson finished.

McDONNELL, in his cross-examination of Robson, concentrated first on his evidence concerning the loaded revolver, which Robson had initially testified was fully loaded. After some discussion of the number of chambers and the number of bullets, it was agreed that two of the cartridges had been dthat the accused had told him that she had got the revolver—which had the name 'Young American' stamped on it—from the manager of the Coogee Beach Hotel. Robson later found out from the manager that this was untrue, although the accused had worked at this hotel as a male useful.

Now McDonnell switched to the matter of identifications in police work, and the possibility of mistaken identity. Robson denied that people were frequently too eager to identify other people as criminals, but admitted that mistakes were often made.

McDonnell had one final question. 'Being largely engaged in the investigation of crime, would you be able to express an opinion on whether the majority or any definite proportions of murderers are run down?'

Coyle objected to this, but Robson answered, 'There are many untraced and many traced—both ways.'

After this question, the case for the Crown was concluded.

AT 2.40 P.M. Eugenia Falleni stood in the dock to make her statement—perceptibly nervous, according to the *Daily Telegraph*.

'Your Honour and gentlemen of the jury, I have been three months in Long Bay Gaol with this terrible charge hanging over my head and I am real nervous—'

Here the judge interjected, asking her to speak up. Her voice, however, was still barely audible as she started again.

> Your Honour, and gentlemen of the jury. I have been three months in Long Bay Gaol and am near a nervous breakdown. I would like to make a statement, but my constitution will not allow me.
>
> I do not know anything at all about this charge. I am perfectly innocent, and do not know what made the woman leave her home. [or, in some newspaper accounts, 'I don't know what the woman done.']
>
> We never had any serious rows, only just a few words, but nothing to speak of, so therefore, I am completely innocent of this charge against me.

Eighteen

ACCORDING to the newspapers, McDonnell, in his address to the jury, produced the rather startling argument that it was not only possible, but probable, that Mrs Birkett was still alive, and in hiding. 'She was in no way at fault, but look at the matter from this point of view', he pronounced:

> 'If a man commits a murder he can live again, and in time become respectable, but if he commits a sexual crime, can he lift his head and ever assume respectability? And if a man became ostracised, what would happen to a woman when her mistake became public?'

He then suggested—perhaps a little contradictorily in view of these remarks—that the Crown had failed to establish a motive.

It was a little after 2.40 p.m. on Wednesday 6 October that McDonnell began his case for the defence. From the court transcripts, the hearing of the defence case seems to have lasted less than an hour, and the burden of the case was an unconvincing attempt to prove that the body may have been misidentified. The testimony was given very little coverage in most of the newspapers, as had been the case with his cross-examination of the prosecution's witnesses. As far as the reporters were concerned, the more practised and flamboyant Coyle obviously made the better copy.

David Horace Love, a manufacturer and a member of the firm of Clifford Love and Co., was the only defence witness called. In 1917 he had been manager of the Chicago Flour Mills at Lane Cove, he told the court. On 26 September, when he was driving in his sulky from the Chicago Flour Mills, he saw a woman walking along, carrying a heavy Japanese wickerwork suitcase. He asked her if she would like a lift—it being a long walk to Chatswood, about three and a half miles—but she did not answer, and walked into the bush. Her attitude, when spoken to, was that of a lunatic, or a half-witted woman.

He added that she wore a dark grey skirt and yellow-coloured coat, and a large 'flop' hat.

The spot where the body was later found was a couple of hundred yards from where the woman had disappeared into the bush, said Love. He saw the woman intermittently over a period of a week, often at about half past five as he returned home. She looked about forty years of age, with grey hair under her big hat, which had a white feather. He believed she might have been camping in the area.

The last time he saw her, he said, was on Thursday 27 September in the evening, when a group of schoolchildren ran up to him, frightened by a woman who had followed them about while they picked wildflowers. He took them in his sulky with him, and saw the woman in the bush at the side of the road. He did not see her again after that date. This was the same evidence he had given at the Coroner's Court on 31 October of that year, 1917, to an inquiry concerning the death of the unknown woman near Chatswood.

To further questions from McDonnell, Love answered that he could not say if the woman wore any jewellery, but her clothing had resembled the exhibits of material he had been shown at the Coroner's Court.

During cross-examination by Coyle, Love admitted that he could not swear to the woman again, having seen her only for a few minutes. He had assumed she had escaped from the lunatic asylum nearby, something that had happened once or twice before. The woman he saw had committed several petty thefts in nearby houses, he was told later, and had since been located.

Love had not made a personal identification of the wandering woman himself, he told McDonnell on further questioning. He had learned she had been found just after the inquest.

McDonnell announced that this closed the case for the defence.

Mr Coyle called on Police Inspector Maze, who had been stationed at Chatswood at the time, to give further evidence about the demented woman wandering in the bush, who had come to police attention by entering houses. As far as he knew, said Maze, the matter had been cleared up. The police were satisfied that the woman had been found living in North Sydney, but as the identification of her was incomplete, they had taken no further action. He repeated that they were satisfied from the description given that this was the woman.

Further cross-examination by McDonnell revealed that Maze had not personally been involved in the matter of the wandering woman. He admitted that then, when his memory was fresher than now, he had been unprepared to say that the descriptions of the woman located at North Sydney and the woman seen wandering in the bush by Love had tallied. The identification, he repeated, had not been complete. This closed the case in reply.

MCDONNELL began his final address to the jury (not given in the court transcripts or reported in detail by the newspapers) at 3.10 in the afternoon and spoke for two hours altogether. During his opening remarks he asked permission to refer to the evidence of one E. M. Hewitt, which had been given in the Police Court proceedings, and Coyle did not object. The accused, on the advice of her counsel, consented to the deposition being read to the jury. This evidence was also not quoted in the court transcripts, but evidently it was to the effect that Miss Hewitt had seen a fire on the Monday in the same direction as the body was found—which would imply that if the victim had been burnt alive by it, she must have been alive on Monday afternoon. If accepted, this would have been in direct conflict with the rest of the forensic evidence, which indicated that the victim had died soon after eating a meal.

After this, at 3.30 p.m., McDonnell resumed his address. Much of it referred to Eugenia's sexuality.

Coyle, the prosecutor, made his own address to the jury at 5.10 p.m., and the Chief Justice began his summing up at 5.38 p.m.

Sir William Cullen, during the proceedings, had been filling his notebook with an angular, almost completely illegible scrawl in black ink. This consisted of a lengthy summary of exhibits: the marriage certificate of Harry Crawford and Annie Birkett; the photographs of Annie; the newspaper with a photograph of Annie's shoes; the shoes themselves and other objects found in the fire; the various photographs taken at the post-mortem; the teeth and the upper plate identified by the dentists McManus and Vernon; the nameplate from the coffin; the police photographs of the site where the body was found; the photographs of the houses in The Avenue, Drummoyne, where Crawford had lived; the linen and cutlery given to Marcellina Bombelli; the diamond ring minded by Lydia Parnell and redeemed from the pawn shop by Frank Bombelli; a photograph of Falleni (here, in the judge's scrawled notes the word 'him' is crossed out and 'her' inserted); the garments given to Henrietta Schieblich; and the statement made by Harry Crawford to Sergeant Robson. Other brief notations concerned McDonnell's (which he spelt 'McDonald's') address to the jury and the possibility of wrong identification, and the confusing issue of E. M. Hewitt's statement.

Having weighed up these various elements in his own mind, Sir William Cullen addressed the gentlemen of the jury for a little over 35 minutes. He began his summary by reminding the jurors that when the Crown laid a criminal charge, it lay with the Crown to prove beyond reasonable doubt that the accused person was guilty of that charge. They must consider carefully the truthfulness of the witnesses, and must not be deterred by the grave consequences of their opinion. They must be judges of fact, nothing more, and it was in this that their duty lay.

If the question depended not on the testimony of eyewitnesses, but on inferences drawn from circumstantial evidence, they must consider that if the facts admitted of any other reasonable explanation consistent with the accused party's innocence, then they were not to convict. In this case, the accused was entitled to the benefit of any doubt.

There were one or two things he wished to mention, continued Cullen. The jury would judge the truthfulness of the witnesses by their demeanour and their lack of inclination to exaggerate. Comment had been made on Mrs Schieblich's impulsiveness, and they must form their own opinion of the reliability of her testimony. As to the accused, even if she had been shown to be deceitful and untruthful, they must not come to the conclusion that she was guilty because of it. They must consider only the evidence concerning the particular offence.

The defence had chiefly discussed the question of the identity of the charred body, Cullen went on. He briefly summarised the evidence concerning the identification—the clothes and minor articles—and the fact that Mrs Birkett had left with the accused in the direction of Lane Cove on that date, and that no one (other than the accused) had claimed to have seen her again after the body was found. They must ask themselves, he told the jury, if the body were not hers, where she would be likely to have gone.

Supposing that they were satisfied that the body was Mrs Birkett's, then the question arose as to whether she was murdered. If death resulted either from a wound inflicted by somebody, or from a fire following that wound, or both, then this would amount to murder. They must consider whether this was how she met her death, or by an accident. If the former, they must consider whether the person who committed that act was the accused.

The jury had heard about the couple's unhappy circumstances, and the seemingly incredible fact that they could live together without Mrs Birkett discovering that a deceit had been practised. Here they must consider the testimony of the other witnesses, such as Mrs Nugent, Annie Birkett's sister, who were also deceived. At all events, the facts seemed to be that the couple were unhappy, that the accused was abusive, and that towards the end of their living together the deception was exposed.

This left the testimony that the two had been seen leaving together on Friday 28 September, and that the accused had later been seen in the area where the body was found. The accused had then told a number of people that Mrs Birkett had left him. The jury should consider how, and if, these accounts threw light on the question.

Cullen concluded his address by repeating his stricture that a theory consistent with guilt was not sufficient. If there were a theory consistent with innocence, then guilt was not established. If, however, after considering all the facts, the jury came to the conclusion that the woman was foully done to death and the person guilty of it was the accused, then their verdict should be guilty.

Cullen asked the jury to consider their verdict.

The jury retired at 6.15 p.m. and returned two hours later, at 8.15 p.m., with a verdict of guilty.

When asked if she had anything to say as to why the sentence of death should not be passed, the accused was understood to say, 'I am not guilty, Your Honour. The jury found me guilty on false evidence. I know nothing about this charge.'

His Honour then passed a sentence of death.

Nineteen

I CLOSED the endless blurred carbon sheets that were the trial transcript and put a rubber band around them. A kaleidoscope of images plucked from the mundane suburban lives of Eugenia's neighbours and acquaintances, they had revealed as much by what was not in them as by what was. Eugenia had said little for herself. The defence counsel had obviously decided that she was an unsafe witness to put in the stand, and allowed her an unconvincing dock statement instead. No alibi was offered, no extenuating version constructed for what might have happened. During her three months of imprisonment before the trial, wrote Moran, Eugenia gave varying accounts of her movements over the period, all of them foolish. Her daughter Josephine was not called upon to testify on her behalf. Maddocks Cohen's efforts in the Police Court to cast doubt on the forensic evidence—changed in nature three years after the events—were rather ineptly pursued by the defence.

Facing Eugenia in the crowded courtroom was the daunting spectacle of the bewigged judge, dressed in scarlet. Her own counsel, in black, was no longer the familiar and experienced Maddocks Cohen, but a new and rather inept younger man, Archie McDonnell. The jury had filed into the box: a handpicked jury of younger men, true, but who could tell how they might react? And in the gallery, the blind, staring face of the rapacious public.

The last day of the trial, Wednesday 6 October 1920, was only a little over a week after the day, three years before, when Eugenia and Annie had set out together for the Lane Cove River. On Oxford Street the people came and went, perhaps aware from the crowd outside that something unusual was happening in the Darlinghurst Courthouse. But the thick sandstone walls and columns kept their counsel for the moment. Inside, insulated, the solemn processes of the law, couched in verbose and archaic language, ran their course. Eugenia sat in the dock, watching in silence, as two men in wigs and gowns argued out her fate. The court stenographers rapidly wrote.

For William Coyle, the prosecutor—experienced, theatrical, meticulous—there was the challenge, perhaps, of an unusual case, but little more. The evidence against the prisoner before him was damning. He would be stern but scrupulously fair, according to his own lights. The outrage that this woman had presented to the established order would work against her any help from him. And he was an honourable man, by reputation, who himself would ascend to the bench a few years later.

'I find it difficult,' he said disingenuously in his opening remarks, 'to refrain from referring to the accused as a man, but when I do, you will understand that I refer to the accused.'

The women in the audience craned to look.

Eugenia: A Man

CONFRONTING Eugenia was a formidable array of male legal expertise. In the highest position was the Honourable Sir William Portus Cullen, KCMG, LLD. William Cullen, despite his father's attempts to impede his education, had risen above his beginnings as the seventh son of an Irish farmer at Mt Johnstone, near Jamberoo, New South Wales, to attain a distinguished academic record. He had been called to the bar in 1883 at the age of 28, and was raised to the bench as Chief Justice in 1910 after a career in Parliament. Now he lived in a stately house, 'Tregoyd', at Balmoral, where, one of the earliest residents to build in the district, he propagated the Australian wildflowers he loved in a bush garden. A strong nationalist and an advocate of law reform, he had been Chancellor of the University of Sydney from 1914. In 1920, when Eugenia faced him, he was a venerable 65 years of age, and had been knighted nine years before, and retirement was not far in front of him.

Arguing against her was the eminent prosecutor W. T. Coyle, KC. Born in Sofala, New South Wales, of parents who had migrated from Northern Ireland, Coyle was called to the bar in England in 1896 and had practised there until he returned to Australia in 1901. Now, with 25 years experience behind him, 'Bulldog' Coyle's appointment as the State's first Senior Crown Prosecutor had been celebrated just a few months before, and he would go on to become a District Court judge in 1927. Knighted in the same year he prosecuted Eugenia, he practised from 176 Phillip Street, Sydney, and gave his residential address in *Who's Who* as Holt Street, Double Bay, higher on the hill near Edgecliff post office. But when

Eugenia was setting out on her laundry cart from Mrs De Angelis's in Pelham Street, only a mile away, Coyle had been pursuing his legal career in London. Immediately after Falleni's trial, Coyle, ever the diplomat, sent an appreciative note to Superintendent Bannan expressing admiration for the way his officers had done their 'difficult duties'. This letter somehow found its way into the *Evening News* of 9 October 1920.

Instead of Maddocks Cohen—shrewd, in his early 50s, descended from an astute Jewish convict made good in Sydney—speaking in Eugenia's defence was junior barrister Mr A. McDonnell of 143 Phillip Street, who apparently did not make a sufficient impression on Chief Justice Sir William Cullen as to allow him to get his name right. Archibald McDonnell had come from Scottish farming stock and made a belated entry to the law at age 42, and was known for an eccentric amateur interest in sexual psychology. However, enthusiasm did not compensate for lack of expertise. Much of his examination of prosecution witnesses seems to a casual observer to have been directionless, even irrelevant—to such a degree that the judge was sufficiently irritated as to interrupt and cut him short, a point not overlooked by the newspapers.

Eugenia Falleni was poor, working class, illiterate, uneducated in the workings of courts and law, and was hardly in a position to stand up for her rights. The police in the lead-up to the trial had put a certain amount of determination into building up their case. One witness, Josephine, they actively discouraged from contacting the defence counsel.

Eugenia Falleni's trial was also characterised, as

murder trials apparently often are, by a number of witnesses who were able to remember in great detail the clothing and appearance of a person they had merely glimpsed, or briefly encountered, three years before, and whom, at the time, they had no particular reason to notice. One, Eliel Irene Carrol, between the Police Court proceedings and the trial, had mysteriously corrected the date of her alleged sighting of Crawford from Sunday to Friday, thus making it more supportive of the police case.

In addition, Mrs Carrol felt able to comment authoritatively that this person's manner had been 'excited or peculiar'—a sure sign of guilt in the eyes of a witness. The defence did little to shake these personal convictions and recollections—which could only have been aided by the numerous newspaper photographs of Eugenia published since her arrest. The jurors in turn would have found it difficult to avoid being influenced by the accompanying press coverage, which had included detailed reporting of testimony not subsequently allowed at the trial.

Worse, many of Crawford's actions since Annie's disappearance had been those of a guilty man with something to hide. Caught out in lies by the police after his arrest, he had merely replaced them with other lies.

The defence put up by McDonnell concentrated largely on the possibility of misidentification of the body—a matter against which the forensic evidence was strong—while not sufficiently highlighting the matter on which the forensic evidence was weak: the likelihood of violence having occurred.

McDonnell seems to have made little of the fact that

the same medical officer who three years previously had positively presented an hypothesis of accidental death, was now brought forward to testify, on the same forensic evidence, that the death was a result of murder. Moran, in his memoir written in the late 1930s, tested the strength of this a little more fully than the defence had done:

> The medical evidence had certain remarkable features. No sign of any depressed fracture was found; nor was there any starring. The extreme degree of heat had completely removed any blood effusion within the skull, if there had been any. It is this tell-tale sign of blood on the inner surface of the cranium that the post-mortem surgeon always looks for in cases of suspected violence. An X-ray photograph of the skull, however, revealed seven linear fractures of which the medical experts thought six were undoubtedly heat effects. The seventh, which was 2 ½ inches in length and situated in the right parietal bone, extended backwards parallel with the squamous suture to end by splitting into two branches. For much of its length it involved the whole bone. The medical witnesses thought this one had been caused by violence. Very fairly they admitted their own doubts about the matter.
>
> Now the subject of skull fractures in persons burnt to death has an extensive literature. Bodies carbonised in the great fires at the Ring Theatre in Vienna (1881) and at the

Eugenia: A Man

Opéra Comique, Paris (1887), still provide
important data. In these cases the fractures
found closely resembled those produced
by a cutting instrument; they were generally fissured like those of Mrs Birkett; and
they were also most frequently found at
the level of the parietal bones. In fact Br-
ouardel, the great French authority, laid
it down that they always occur there.

No medical expert was called for the defence.

Had one been available it would have been
possible at the very least, to impair the value
of the medical opinions offered for the prosecution. These same experts had three years
before positively declared that there were no
signs of violence. ... They very fairly admitted doubt about the cause of the seventh
fracture. But it really did seem a little dar-
ing in the presence of an efficient cause for
linear skull fractures (which was the fire) to
say even in the mildest of dogmatic man-
ners, 'these six, we are sure, were caused by
heat alone, that one, there, by violence.'

The Crown Prosecutor reconstruct-
ing the crime pictured Falleni stunning
the recumbent victim into unconsciousness by means of some blunt weapon.

Only Falleni knows what really happened.

A forensic expert I consulted in May 1986 also gave an opinion. On the evidence available, he told me that if the fracture to the skull had been caused by a blow sufficient to induce unconsciousness, signs of internal haemorrhage should have been apparent when the skull was opened at the first post-mortem, despite the external burning.

Twenty

THE Australian Year Book of 1919 describes the women's prison at Long Bay, opened ten years before, as 'a well-designed reformatory for females'. Recent innovations included the then revolutionary concept of segregating prisoners according to the seriousness of their crimes, and 'reform rather than retribution' was a stated aim. A random survey of the surviving records reveals that many of the women who passed through its gates were little more than minor casualties of a society where respectability in women was prized.

The photographic record books in the State Archives display an endless succession of haunted, often simpleminded faces of young girls and lined and battered older women. The names are sometimes Aboriginal, sometimes Irish. Some of the women are described as being in domestic service, more often they are unemployed. Usually they have little education. The crimes they have committed are often crimes against the accepted female role: vagrancy (the sin of being without a home); drunkenness, riotous behaviour and indecent language (the sin of being 'unladylike'), and 'creating a nuisance' (a euphemism for prostitution). Others have been convicted of petty theft of the type that usually accompanies poverty: pickpocketing, shoplifting, and stealing from places of employment by servant girls. For crimes like these, some of the women have over a hundred convictions.

The more serious offences include assault, receiving stolen goods, passing false cheques and—very occasionally—manslaughter (often middle-aged women whose other convictions suggest that they were abortionists).

The great majority of women passing through the reformatory in the early 1920s were serving minor sentences, some of only 24 hours or a few days, others of a few weeks or months. In this rogues' gallery, the female murderers stand out in their scarcity.

Eugenia also left her fleeting mark in the ponderous Department of Corrective Service ledgers: large, bound volumes such as the Entrance and Discharge books for the State Reformatory for Women, Long Bay. As late as 1921 these still had columns bearing the convict legend 'Ship and Date of Arrival', now crossed out and amended to 'Place of Birth'. These enigmatic entries do little but affirm that, yes, on such-and-such a date Eugenia was allowed to exit or readmitted through these gates during her hearings and trial, among the endless stream of women arrested for petty crimes, each marked off by the same deliberate nib of an unknown clerk, each entry representing a life story equally unknowable.

The last red ink notation in the Entrance book for Eugenia (entry 1012), dated 6 October, reads 'Sentenced to death'. Underneath, a different hand has noted in black ink '1st timer' and 'appealed 9 October 1920'. And underneath that in yet another ink (this time a washed-out pink) are the words, 'leave to appeal refused by High Court, conviction affirmed'. On 12 November 1920, we may learn, Justices Pring, Ferguson and Wade of the Court of Criminal Appeal dismissed Falleni's appeal, holding that if the jury had concluded that the accused was the person who brought about the victim's death, no matter by what means, the jury was justified in finding a verdict of guilty.

On 6 December 1920 the matter of Falleni's death sentence was discussed in the State Cabinet, and on the same day the sentence was commuted to Penal Servitude for Life. The last page of the photograph/description album, labelled 'Females, Long Bay, No. 3'—buckled, tattered and disintegrating in its webbing straps—contains Entry 499:

> Name: *Eugene Falleni*
> Date when Portrait taken: *21 Oct 1920*
> Native Place: *Italy*
> Date of Birth: *25/7/1875*[7]
> Trade or occupation: *Hotel Useful*
> Religion: Roman *Catholic*
> Education, degree of: *nil*[8]
> Height without shoes: *5ft 4 ins*
> Weight in lbs (on committal): *126 lbs*
> Colour of hair: *dark brown*
> Colour of eyes: *blue*
> Marks or special features: *little finger missing R. hand*

---

[7] In fact, 25 January 1875.

[8] Most of the other entries in this category state 'read and write'.

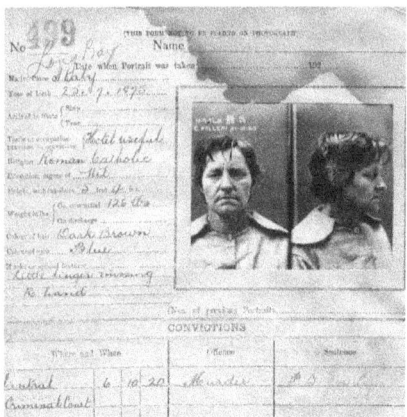

Eugenia was photographed for the prison records on 21 October 1920, ten days after she had been sentenced to death and nearly four months after her arrest. At this time, her sentence had not yet been commuted to penal servitude for life, and leave to appeal had been refused. Photo: Archives Authority of NSW, by permission of the Department of Corrective Services

The person pictured beside this description, in what looks like a rough cotton prison uniform with a broad, round collar, is, to all impressions, female. In the three months since her arrest, Eugenia's hair has grown longer and more straggly, but the face is unmistakably that of a middle-aged woman with regular, handsome features and a turned-down mouth. Her eyes—usually shaded under a man's hat in the newspaper photographs—are creased downwards at the lids and gaze steadily outwards with an expression somewhere between grief and resignation. The profile shows grey in the hair brushed untidily back over the ears. The weathered face is wrinkled around the eyes, with deep frown lines between the eyebrows and deep creases running from the nose to the outer corners of the mouth. Looking at the photograph one is forced to wonder, even allowing for the longer hair, how Eugenia could ever have been taken for a man.

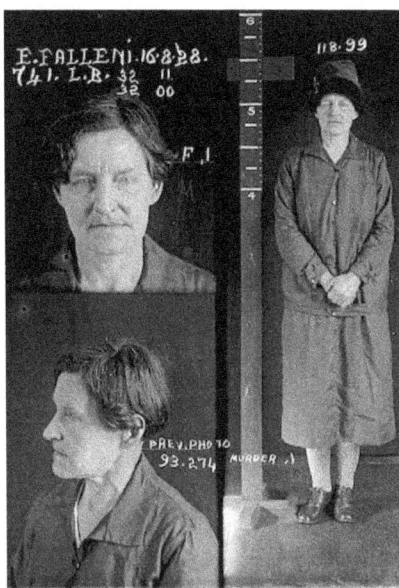

On 16 August 1928, after eight years in prison, Eugenia again faced the prison photographer. She would be released three years later, on 18 February 1931. Photo: State Reformatory for Women. Photo description books. State Records New South Wales, by permission of the Department of Corrective Services

ON 16 AUGUST 1928, some seven years later, Eugenia was photographed again. In the succeeding album, entry 741 repeats the same personal details, but the accompanying set of images is completely different. Now Eugenia is very much thinner, and the lines on her face are even more deeply etched. Her pale eyes seem to stare defiantly at the observer, and now the face looks harder in its expression, the features more strictly controlled. Only the set of the mouth in the profile shot seems to convey the anxiety apparent in the earlier pictures. Included is a full-length portrait that shows the prisoner in a shapeless woman's dress, buttoned down the front from a plain collar, belted low on the hips and reaching to mid-calf. She wears thick, textured stockings and flat lace-up shoes, and on her head is a shapeless hat that resembles a padded tea cosy. It is difficult not to be led into a comparison of this frowzy woman with the infinitely smarter and better-tailored male figure she presented at her committal.

Eugenia behaved well in prison. Her name does not appear in the Punishment Book, among those of other female convicts who sent out clandestine letters, assaulted or abused fellow prisoners, made false statements, were disobedient or insolent, or who quarrelled or fought, and were duly sent before the magistrate to be cautioned, reprimanded or admonished, or sent to the cells for several days or a week.

Harry Cox, an ex-policeman, in his recollections in 1961, remembered her in 1928 as a 'serene, grey-haired woman', enjoying her work in the prison flower gardens—characteristically, outdoor work that she could perform in solitude.

However, her name crops up repeatedly in the 'Record of Cases treated in the Gaol Hospital'. On 20 June 1921 Eugenia complained of backache and spent two weeks in hospital before being released to 'A Hall' on 3 July. From 17 to 29 November 1921 she was again in the hospital, but no details were entered of her complaint. In 1922 she was discharged on 11 February after an unknown period in hospital suffering from 'debility'.

Around April 1922 Eugenia, now referred to as

Eugenia: A Man

'Jean', underwent an unspecified operation at 'C' Hospital. (This referred to Prince Henry Hospital, a little further down Anzac Parade, then known as the Coast Hospital. Here, in July 1921, another isolated figure who had battled alcoholism and depression in cheap boarding houses around Sydney had been admitted to fight the cerebral haemorrhage that would kill him within a year. This was the poet and writer Henry Lawson.) For Eugenia, further periods of hospitalisation for unspecified complaints began on 22 March 1928, on 20 March 1929, on 1 July 1929 and on 1 June 1930.

A CAMPAIGN to free Eugenia began in 1928 and continued through 1929, partly as an adjunct to efforts to win freedom for another high profile woman prisoner, Dorothy Mort. A middle-class married woman from Lindfield on Sydney's North Shore, Mrs Mort, aged 36, had been tried for murder in April 1921 after shooting dead her younger lover Dr Claude Tozer, and then almost fatally wounding herself, after he told her he intended to marry another. Mort—erratic, tormented and deluded—was found not guilty on the ground of insanity and detained at the Governor's pleasure. After nine years of incarceration, and with medical opinion now holding that she was sane, a group of socially prominent people had got up a petition for her release.

On 7 July 1929 the Sunday News, raising the possibility that Falleni was innocent and calling for an inquiry into her conviction, compared her lot— 'without hope, utterly friendless, and by the world forgot'—with Mrs Mort's, whose influential 'friends' were working tirelessly for her discharge. Mort was finally freed in October the same year.

According to the *Sun* of 14 August 1954, in a recap of the events, Eugenia was now a 'broken, pitiful creature deserving of sympathy and mercy', and 'various people had interested themselves in her plight'. The debate gave the weekly scandal sheets *Truth* and *Smith's Weekly* an excuse to launch into one of their customary skirmishes: *Smith's* championing the 'battler' allegedly hounded by the authorities and with the world against her; while *Truth*—as guardian of public morality and rectitude (especially when its campaigns could be accompanied by as much salacious detail as possible)—took the opposite view.

On Saturday 8 March 1930 *Smith's*—under the headline MAN-WOMAN EUGENE FALLENI MAKES APPEAL FOR FREEDOM: TELLS HER POIGNANT STORY TO 'SMITH'S WEEKLY'—devoted its entire front page to a piteous account of how 'Today Eugene Falleni, pink handkerchief in her gnarled hand, makes a humble, feminine gesture of entreaty.' Falleni, the paper contended, was now regarded as a model prisoner, feminine and harmless, and did not want to die in gaol.

Eugenia: A Man

Smith's Weekly Saturday 8 March 1930 Photo: State Library of NSW

On Sunday 16 March 1930, a week later, *Truth* retaliated with FIENDISH MAN-WOMAN, MURDERESS—SHOULD BE NO MISPLACED SYMPATHY FOR DESPICABLE HUMAN MONSTER. The paper reported that a 'shocked' Harry Birkett was strongly opposed to her release, and accused her of changing 'only her vocabulary' in presenting herself as a 'crushed and martyred spirit'.

Truth Sunday 16 March 1930. Photo: State Library of NSW

By Sunday 10 August, however, having evidently sent a journalist to visit the prison, *Truth* had changed its tune. 'The day starts early at the Bay. At 4.30 a.m. an army of women with buckets and scrubbing brushes, polishing clothes and dusters, answers the roll call,' it began. Falleni—'a broken woman convicted on circumstantial evidence'—had for ten years worked in the cookhouse, but after the release of Dorothy Mort, was apparently promoted to her position in the library, and now worked a few hours only. Eugenia, claimed *Truth*, was said to be more popular than Dorothy, who 'gave herself airs'.

'Falleni is an old woman without hope,' the paper finished. 'If she is released now she will be fit only for an old women's home or a hospice.'

After a personal visit to the gaol by the new NSW Labor Justice Minister Joe Lamaro in November 1930, Eugenia was granted conditional release on 19 February 1931 on compassionate grounds, due to her age, state of health and good behaviour. Among the school of minor offenders with sentences ranging from 24 hours to three months, Eugenia stands out as the only apparent 'lifer' discharged in the period.

According to *Truth*, after her release Eugenia was taken in by 'a wealthy woman living at Lindfield, who has on previous occasions interested herself in well-known prisoners, [and] has given the queer old woman shelter.'

The temptation to think that this might be Dorothy Mort, who had evidently befriended Eugenia in prison, and (according to one apparently erroneous newspaper story) had taught her to read and write while both worked in the prison library, is probably mistaken: after her release, Mort lived very privately with her husband and children in Mosman.

Twenty-One

TODAY, when you drive out along Anzac Parade, the watchtowers and tall, purple-brown brick buildings of Long Bay are visible from some distance. The prison, some miles south of the city, and insulated from the public road by windy open spaces and a high, barbed-wire topped fence, is built on a flat, unsheltered headland with Botany Bay on one side and the Pacific Ocean on the other. A little further on is a small sandy beach surrounded by sparse grass and sand drifts. Here, 200 years ago, Jean François de la Perouse sheltered his French ships before sailing away to be wrecked in the New Hebrides.

If you walk along the headland you will find, beside a sandstone gun turret, the traditional snake man in his corrugated iron arena, displaying with studied carelessness his brown snakes and tiger snakes to the tourists. A little further on an old part-Aboriginal man demonstrates the throwing of boomerangs, a remnant of the days when a larger community of Aborigines still lived at La Perouse. Not far away is the little suburb of Matraville, named after James Mario Matra, who came with Captain Cook on his first voyage of exploration, the first Italian to reach Australia.

Eugenia: A Man

But Eugenia, tending the salty and windswept flower and vegetable gardens behind the prison walls of Long Bay Gaol, would have cared little for these historical associations. On a rainy day, the gaol seems particularly cold and unsheltered as you approach the security check at the wire fence. The entrance is reached by an arcade of ancient and sombre palm trees which runs beside a solid wall of mossy sandstone and dun bricks. Then there is the daunting gatehouse, guarded by rampant lion and unicorn, and crowned by sandstone turrets and an ornate copper-decorated and slate-tiled roof.

Nowadays the gate itself is corrugated steel, with a one-way mirror observation slit set in a smaller door. This door opens no more than is necessary to allow entry and shuts rapidly with a clang. There are no women inmates at Long Bay now, but most of the visitors are little groups of women; mothers and wives and girlfriends, defiantly well-dressed, frowning or anxious or stolid as they stump along the rain-wet asphalt.

In the distance, seagulls screech above the new brick suburbs and industrial landscape, and the sea behind is a flat, metallic grey. Perhaps it was just a product of the rain, but I found it hard not to leave the place feeling morose and depressed.

HERBERT Moran went to see Eugenia in prison twice, and she twice visited him after her release in February 1931. The doctor, oddly enough, had been persuaded to visit the prisoner by William Coyle, the Crown Prosecutor who had succeeded in sending Eugenia to Long Bay Gaol. Coyle knew Moran spoke

Italian and thought that being able to converse in her own language—Eugenia apparently still spoke a Tuscan dialect—would comfort her. It was typically eccentric of Coyle—who would later gain respect as a criminal court judge—to successfully prosecute Eugenia, and then send associates and friends, including his wife, to visit and comfort her.

Moran had been given a pass to enter the prison by Justice Minister W. J. McKell, MLA, and on a sunny day in 1929 he made his first trip out to Malabar. The fortress-like buildings of Long Bay Gaol were that day backed by a wind-whipped ocean. Moran felt quite cheerful until he reached the iron gates of the prison. However, on entering, the prisoners he saw seemed dull-eyed and dejected, and their 'brooding hopelessness' appalled him. He also commented in his memoir on the 'hard iron eyes' of the prison guards, but hypothesised a little idealistically that this might be a defence against pity. Their faces, he wrote, bore the marks of alcoholic abuse.

Moran waited in an uncomfortable chair in the company of a prison matron until Eugenia was brought to him.

> She came in shyly and suspiciously, a woman of fifty-four years. The stature was short and the gait slouching. She still seemed to be deliberately exaggerating the stride of a man. The grey eyes were restless and afraid; the face olive-tinted, lined, hairless. Such a head would easily pass for a man's. Her hair was indeed still short. It was brushed straight back and there were patches of grey. The nose was thick

> and undistinguished. She was flat in the bust. The voice was low-pitched and raucous, the manner subservient but distrustful. Obviously her intellect was fixed permanently in low gear. The hands were large and spade-like, suggesting those of a manual labourer.

Looking at it from her side, the illiterate Eugenia, now in her mid fifties, was confronted with a 44-year-old, well-dressed professional man, an envoy of those who had imprisoned her, who further confused her by speaking to her in educated Italian. This stranger claimed that he wished to help her in any way he could, and may have asked if she would like to return Italy, a country she had left at the age of two. Eugenia, no doubt worn down and conditioned by nearly ten years of prison life, reacted with caution and guardedness.

It was the monotony, she told him, that was the worst of it. She said she was in Long Bay Gaol 'only on suspicion'—something she may have convinced herself to believe, having been instructed to plead not guilty, and no doubt having little knowledge of the processes of law. It may equally likely have been a conscious lie. She continued to protest her innocence, but in a tone that the doctor found unconvincing. She remained guarded in her manner, watching the man opposite her carefully, but making no apparent bid for sympathy. 'At no time then or later,' wrote Moran, 'did she try to dramatise herself.'

Moran was not impressed with Eugenia's intellectual capacities. He concluded that she was 'just a half-wild creature who felt herself apart and different'. He went on to comment on her far removal from those 'Sapphic' women celebrated by Dante. (It would not be until the 1940s that distinctions between homosexuality, transvestism, and transsexualism became widely accepted in medical and scientific circles. Moran, in his account, equates Eugenia's state with lesbianism.)

Eugenia was aggressively masculine in neither manner nor appearance, the doctor wrote. He concluded that she was largely motivated in life by fear. Reading between the lines, the good doctor may have been a little disappointed by her ordinariness.

IT WAS the monotony that was the worst of it.

At the time of her sentencing in 1920, Eugenia was in little danger of being hanged. Between 1900 and 1920 a total of 54 women and 256 men were tried for murder in New South Wales, but of the women, only a dozen or so were convicted. In 1920 no women were executed in New South Wales, and one in South Australia in that year was the total for the nation.

In the last decade of the previous century, Frances Knorr had been hanged in Melbourne on 15 January 1894, after becoming involved in a racket that dealt with unwanted babies. She would collect the infant and a payment from the mother, and then dispose of the baby by battering it to death. On 22 October of the same year, Martha Needle, who had insured and then murdered various members of her family, was also hanged in Melbourne. Louisa Collins, in January 1889, was hanged in New South Wales after poisoning two husbands, also for the insurance money. I could find nothing in the records of women executed in

New South Wales after 1900.

However, from the same records, between 1921 and 1929, apart from Eugenia Falleni and Dorothy Mort, two other women did time in Long Bay for murder. One was Sara Boyd, aged 29, who was convicted on 20 December 1923 for strangling another woman's unwanted baby, fathered by Boyd's brother, which she was looking after at the time. Sara subsequently threw the body, in a suitcase, off a ferry, after which members of a Sunday school picnic found it on a nearby beach. Sara Boyd was sentenced to death, with the sentence subsequently commuted to life imprisonment.

The other was Emily Hemsworth, 24, of Muswellbrook, who in March 1925 was accused of murdering her four-week-old baby, after the child's father, a married dairy farmer with seven children, for whom Emily had evidently worked without pay, told her not to bring it home. Unable to remember any details of the killing, she had left the body wrapped in brown paper on the train back to Muswellbrook, and was found not guilty of infanticide on the ground of insanity.

According to Moran, in gaol Eugenia engaged in a relationship—a 'ridiculous little sentimental liaison'—with another female prisoner convicted of murder, whose story was equally bizarre. Which of these alleged murderesses may have been the object of Eugenia's affection he does not reveal.

'She went always, even there, aloof, although her snarling moods grew rare', Moran wrote of Eugenia in prison. 'Some sort of peace came upon her, although the old fires were only banked down. Sometimes, indeed, they flared balefully.'

H. M. MORAN, an educated man and a religious one, much-travelled in England, France and Italy, who scattered literary allusions through his memoirs and titled them with tags from Shakespeare, starts his chapter on Eugenia by openly describing his own revulsion at male homosexuality, a revulsion he believes is instinctive.

He conjectures that it may be a 'biological aversion', an explosion of hostility of the 'race continuers' for the 'race destroyers'. He admits that weight is lent to this by 'social, moral and aesthetic prejudices'. He wonders if his own disgust may in fact be rooted in his schooldays, when two boys were expelled for some 'mischief' in a lavatory. In his subsequent encounters with male homosexuals he describes them in highly unflattering terms, although he is a little puzzled at having come across—or perhaps recognised—so few: especially as he has heard police reports that 150 men had been arrested over a two-year period for homosexual offences in a single lavatory in Hyde Park in Sydney.

Moran conjectures that a puritan Catholic atmosphere, such as that of his own upbringing, could create a distorted and unhealthy idea of heterosexual sex, and that 'perverse and irregular habits' might have their origin in the conflict caused by those same rigid moral precepts. He even seems a little disapproving (as a man of science) of his own intolerance.

He then rather naïvely contradicts his earlier hypothesis (for surely homosexual women are as much 'race destroyers' as homosexual men?) by stating that he has no such feelings against the same trait in women:

> But if the horror I feel for male inversion remains intense, I feel strangely tolerant towards women given to homosexuality and can bring to the subject a detached, even a sympathetic attitude. Of course, in all disease this should be the habitual approach of a medical observer. The world certainly views this womanly conduct more leniently. The Church in former ages regarded it merely as venial sin. Why this is all so, it is difficult to explain.

Despite his preconceptions, Moran's account provides the only clues available to Eugenia's sexuality. He does not suggest at any point that she had sexual encounters with men apart from 'Martello', the alleged father of Josephine, and presumably he would have made reference to them if he had knowledge of them. He does note, however, that at some point in her life Eugenia became sexually active with women.

According to Moran, unpublished records of the case reveal that Harry Crawford had at one stage simultaneously wooed two married women who lived next door to each other. Intensely jealous, one of them was reduced to boring a hole in the weatherboard wall of her neighbour's house to spy on her lover's infidelities. Neither woman seemed to be aware that Harry was not a man.

Harry had constructed a phallus, (the 'article' referred to in the court proceedings, which Moran described as 'a miserable thing, of dirty rags covered with gauze and capped with rubber'), harnessed it to his body, and none of his lovers apparently knew the difference. One of the married women, wrote Moran, who supplied information to police on condition that she not be subpoenaed as a witness, fainted when confronted with it.

According to Moran, Harry's second wife, Lizzie Allison, a Scotswoman of over fifty and a spinster prior to her marriage, had flatly refused to accept what she was told by police after Harry's arrest. At that time, she believed that she was pregnant to Harry—a delusion evidently caused by the physiological symptoms of menopause, which Moran claimed sometimes deceived women and doctors alike, and which had unfortunately coincided with the events. Loyal and obstinate, wanting Harry back, Lizzie held out until confronted with the 'object' which the detectives had found in the locked trunk, and which they would later put in the Police Museum in Sydney labelled 'Article 35'.

Harry, surmised Moran, had evolved a technique that only the sexual mores of the day could have made possible: drawn blinds, an extinguished light, and in the darkened bedroom an assumption of modesty, and retirement alone before and after the act, so that his wives and mistresses never saw him entirely unclothed or uncovered. He would have been well grounded in the tricks of concealing his body without making it appear obvious from his days among sailors in the crowded fo'c'sle seventeen years before.

H. M. Moran gives some emphasis to this apparatus in his account, as did Coyle in his prosecution. That Harry seems to have had relationships with a number of women over a period of time, apparently inspiring both love and jealousy, might indicate a high level of sexual activity. It seems to me just as likely, however, that Crawford kept physical lovemaking to a minimum and relied on the emotional aspects of the relationship to maintain the involvement. Whatever the case, one is led to wonder what repeatedly drove Eugenia to engage in these dangerous charades with women, where discovery would have been disastrous. Nevertheless, Harry's lovers demonstrated a remarkable capacity to believe what they wished to believe. Harry Crawford was in later life apparently neither physically beautiful nor handsome in the accepted sense, and Moran repeatedly demeans his intelligence. Despite this, two women at least, as well as his second wife, were in love with him.

What seems to have been overlooked by previous commentators on Eugenia's story is the extent to which it affirms the fierceness of the human need for love.

PART TWO

Publish such histories, even if they are just sketches. It is a realm of great wonder.

> —A. R. LURIA, neurologist,
> in a letter to Dr Oliver Sacks

Twenty-Two

WHAT was I hoping to achieve, I wondered, by trying to deduce Eugenia from dry scraps of paper, aged official documents and sensational newspaper accounts, all of which represented their own form of fiction? Was it possible to build a construct from the outside, and hope that the shape which resulted might somehow correspond with the shape that was Eugenia?

And yet, it seemed to me, no aspiring biographer, no matter how skilled, can define a person, once they are dead, beyond the traces they have made in the material world. With more self-conscious subjects, and those with an eye on posterity, these traces are often the ones they wish to leave. With Eugenia this was also true, and yet not true at all.

Eugenia wished to be a man called Harry Crawford in the eyes of the world, and this despite the pressure of a then universally prevailing belief that, born a woman, she should have lived as one. The man she had created herself as was psychologically convincing in his own right: a working man with the rough habits of his milieu; the dependence on alcohol that might have come from his rum-drinking days at sea and his time in the hotels of Sydney, and the attitude to his female companions that was typical of his day. And yet, behind this man was a being who had done, what was in her time, the almost unimaginable.

Should I be admiring of Eugenia's brave disregard of the sex for which the world, her family, and the accident of her birth, had predestined her? Or was Eugenia, more than any other human being a victim, hounded throughout her life by her own ambivalent nature?

And how, if at all, did this ambivalent condition contribute to Annie Birkett's death?

The pile of papers, notes and copies of newspaper articles were scattered all over my study. I left them there, stymied. Eugenia was unapproachable, and there was still no key to what had actually happened.

In the autumn of 1986, however, I went over them yet again. If Eugenia had ever been master of her own destiny, by the time she was in her early forties, and in prison, that control had slipped from her hands. And yet, nowhere so far had she confessed to the crime of which she was convicted, nor confided in anyone.

THERE had been others besides me who found the events of Eugenia's trial unsatisfactory.

'The trial and conviction of that abnormal woman, Eugene Falleni, raises speculation regarding the duty of the Crown, when an accused person without money is charged with a capital offence,' wrote an anonymous correspondent in *Smith's Weekly* on 9 October 1920.

Eugenia: A Man

> To marshal evidence against Falleni, the
> Crown selected Mr Coyle, a most ex-
> perienced barrister with an unsurpassed
> reputation as a successful prosecutor.
>
> To weaken the evidence in its doubt-
> ful phases, and to prove 'the benefit of the
> doubt' for the accused, the Crown chose
> Mr McDonnell, a junior barrister, with
> no special reputation in the defence of
> persons charged with serious crime.
>
> There are ways in which the Crown can give
> a fairer run to persons on trial for their lives.

In his opinion, the writer concluded, the Crown had not given Falleni an even chance.

In the following week *Smith's Weekly*, an eccentric paper founded after World War I by Sir James Joynton Smith, once again took an interest. This time one of its columnists, under the nom de plume 'The Man in the Mask', commented on the case in an article entitled 'The Falleni Tragedy'. This dissertation filled two and a half tabloid-length columns, and was set off by the *Weekly*'s usual assembly of advertisements for patent medicines, doggerel verse, one-line jokes and irreverent cartoons.

A friend, 'a retired god' (an ex-barrister or judge perhaps?) had taken the writer to a strange concert— the trial—to witness 'the music of life', wrote the Man in the Mask.

In his subsequent examination of one 'note' in this symphony, the anonymous contributor hypothesised that Falleni's body had formed a battleground for her own 'young soul' against an intruder described as 'the ghoulish wraith of some unclean ancestor'.

> The body was a house divided—a misused mansion—an ugliness where nature hid its naked beauty in a rage of bestiality.
>
> The dwelling that had been designed for the sacred ceremonies of motherhood became a ribald clubhouse for mock rites of masculinity.
>
> The cowering soul-thing was forced to witness these rites, even to participate in them, and instead of being able to witness the clean ecstasy of life, it had to content itself with suffocating gusts of falsehood.
>
> So it was that a pathetic figure, longing to be a man, because it knew itself no longer a woman, went nervously through the days, doubly afraid of the loneliness that all souls fear, and seeking by sly means to win companionship, and to satisfy the fantastic curiosity of the ghoul that ruled it.

At one stage of Falleni's trial, the author continued, Coyle, in what seems like an act of gratuitous theatre, 'with practised dramatic gesture and well ordered disgust ... cast before the eyes of her judges ... the grotesque symbol of her distorted longings' (presumably the 'article', or artificial phallus).

Now he sketched in a few colourful details—the

'unseemly scarlet robes' of the judge; the 'tragic calm' of Falleni herself; the gazes of the curiosity-seekers as Coyle's 'incisive and powerful' voice 'declaimed against her'; the 'portly female witness' (possibly the neighbour Mrs Gough, portrayed in newspapers as aggressive and voluble in delivering her evidence); the 'yawning juror'—before ending on a note of what for the first time sounded like genuine compassion for the 'poor wretch' so caught up in circumstances beyond her control.

NEWSPAPERS had played an important role in the dissemination of news about the trial. Their stories varied according to their motives and their readerships. In days before television and radio soap operas and live news coverage, these day-by-day press accounts of popular scandals, crimes and divorces probably fulfilled much the same function. Two other long-running sagas of the period—a controversy over the proposed deportation of Father Charles Jerger, who had been jailed in wartime as an enemy alien, and who in commenting on conscription was said to have uttered pro-German sentiments; and the escape from a convent at Wagga of a pregnant nun, Sister Ligouri, and the subsequent attempts by police to 'rescue' her—were simultaneously given lengthy coverage.

At the time of the trial, the *Sunday Truth*'s treatment of the Falleni story had been remarkably restrained, considering the paper's evident enjoyment of scandal-mongering. Typically, on 10 October 1920, as well as listing the latest attraction from Hoyts' 'Theatre de Luxe' in George Street—described as 'The Heart of Humanity: A Stirring Tale of Mother Love'—it also published a lengthy story headed 'Black Trash: Britain's Coloured Menace'—the main burden of which seemed to be the fascination of English women on all levels of society with 'American Negroes', particularly bandleaders.

Truth assigned almost a full page in this issue to the court proceedings, with only advertisements filling the remaining space. The story restricted itself to a lengthy summary of the evidence, although little of it was devoted to the defence. By some odd streak of irony, the largest ad—almost a quarter page—was for 'Palmerite Tailoring, Makers of Quality Menswear'.

The respectable dailies, the *Sydney Morning Herald* and the Melbourne *Age*, true to type, gave the trial a series of six-inch columns on an inside page, densely packed and factual. Both were understandably much more concerned with the concurrent visit of the Prince of Wales.

However, the end of the trial, and Eugenia's sentencing, did not mark the end of press interest in her case. At various times over the next six decades, her story would be hauled out of the files and caricatured in publications such as the *Sun*, *Truth*, *Sunday Mirror*, *Australasian Post*, *Daily Mirror* and *Adam*. With time, the condemnatory assumptions and exaggerations would increase. Eugenia, an 'incorrigible lesbian', would be portrayed as having brutally battered Annie Birkett to death with a rock as she bent innocently over a picnic basket, and then (a considerable feat for one of her size) hurling the body on to a huge bonfire of logs lit with kerosene. The incidents at Watson's Bay and Bellevue Hill would become increasingly lurid, and Eugenia would be repeatedly characterised as violent, foul-mouthed and drunken; an exploiter of naïve women and a smoker of foul-smelling cigars who was always ready to fight with her fists. Her exploits at sea would reach unlikely proportions and her time on board ship be extended to six years.

By the time the story reached the *World News* magazine on 11 September 1954, accompanied by a garish line drawing of a large, muscular man brandishing a rock over a frail and beautiful blonde woman, Eugenia's career had been extended to logger and station-hand, the number of her marriages to three, and she was described in prison (with no foundation that can be readily established) as 'a constant source of trouble to the authorities due to her sadistic and twisted sexual outlook'. Another writer, Englishman Leonard Gribble, in a collection of crime stories entitled *Hallmark of Horror*, called her a 'monster', an 'amalgam of deformed humans', and a hermaphrodite.

This type of story was mainly perpetuated by male 'crime writers', but Patricia Gifney, in a series in the *Sun* called 'Women in Crime', was content to rehash the same inaccurate material as late as 26 February 1971.

A more honourable if equally unreliable effort was produced by *Smith's Weekly* on 25 June 1938, under Kenneth Slessor's editorship, when Eugenia was again a subject of newspaper stories. The paper's 'medical writer' commented on similar cases throughout history, in particular, on 'Bill Smith', a milk carter from Parramatta who had also worked as a timber getter, selector, horse trainer and station hand, and who, when discovered to be a woman in 1932, had lived as a man for twenty years. The writer went on to present a theory about a 'chemical' process that allegedly controlled sexuality:

> Though sex is determined at the moment of conception, a chemical control takes over its maintenance in the period before birth. For a baby-boy there is one definite chemical, for a baby-girl, another, different in containing one less atom of carbon, and five less of hydrogen.
>
> Through some defect, sometimes a baby-girl develops the male chemical in the period before birth.

However, this writer ended on a puzzling note:

> Falleni made a clean breast of the facts at her trial. Her story was that, after a violent quarrel, she killed her 'wife' in a fit of passion; and, seized with panic, attempted to destroy the body. But probably influenced by the sex factor in the case, judge and jury rejected the plea of homicide. Falleni was found guilty of murder and sentenced to death ...

At my desk in Sydney, I reflected that even today a psychologist would probably tabulate Eugenia's condition in cold clinical terms that made her every act explicable, even predictable, with any mystery being discounted.

Sometimes it is possible to capture a certain accidental conjunction of ideas that emerges from a mass of facts: one of those small moments of illumination which, when it occurs, makes you think you might be on the verge of a discovery. But then nothing further happens. The more banal details of life crowd out the perception: the low grey buzz of existence fogs it over as the inadequate mechanism of the brain copes with the next eventuality. With Eugenia, any such discovery was going to prove doubly elusive, I suspected, but I wondered if it might have something to do with the nature of freedom.

Every child has a great curiosity as to how the world works. Whether the world is really the orderly, regulated place that adults present to them, or whether it is (as children secretly suspect) chaotic. Children know that what they think and feel, and what it is allowable for them to think, are two different things. They wonder if, beneath the careful exteriors, everyone senses the same dichotomy.

Gradually, like all children, they forget the chaos, and learn by imitation enough behaviour patterns and mannerisms to get by, until the things learnt gradually become indistinguishable from the truth, and they no longer worry about the duality. They forget the world as they first experienced it, although they might remember that such a world existed.

Eugenia, on the other hand, grew up without developing the requisite set of rules and beliefs about being a woman—or was able to resist adopting them. Doubtless she developed an equally crippling set of assumptions about the way she should live as a male. But it was only in the rejection of her 'natural' set of mores that her freedom lay. (For, second only to our species, what is more fundamental than our biological maleness and femaleness?)

Eugenia, a woman, became invisible to men. Men, unwary, believing she was a man, would have hid little from her. A mole, she penetrated the great male conspiracy as no other woman could (just as no man can penetrate the great female conspiracy). Yet, what did it matter to her, this involuntary spy, if it was never a desire of hers to return to her own camp?

In payment for this form of freedom, Eugenia spent her life trying to keep chaos at bay while following an uncharted course. She never told anyone what she had learnt, never wrote it down; never, probably, even pondered on it. She merely went on with her life as she felt she must.

Why was I asking more of her? What more *could* one ask?

Only that, how else can we define this chaos we have so carefully taught ourselves not to recognise, except by glimpses through the eyes of those who have put themselves outside the comfortable world? How else can we learn to recognise freedom?

What I was trying to do, as I sat in my paper-covered study in a well-mannered suburb, was solve a murder in retrospect—although perpetrator and victim were long since identified and dealt with by the courts, and Eugenia Falleni herself was long since dead. The story, I was convinced, had not been told—not by the contemporary newspapers; not by the court transcripts; not by the honest doctor who had known Eugenia and who in his written account had tried to grapple with the facts of her life; and least of all by the crime reporters who had so brutally and inaccurately sensationalised her tragedy for the evening tabloid readers at intervals in the fifty years since it had occurred.

Twenty-Three

THE WELLINGTON telephone book revealed six numbers under the name Falleni. A friend, a journalist on a visit to New Zealand, typed them out, along with the addresses, and brought them back for me. I hesitated for a while. Until now I had been playing detective for my own amusement. It was one thing to shuffle papers harmlessly in libraries and archives, another to venture into the real world. Living relatives of Eugenia might not wish to know of her, or of me.

After several attempts, I finally composed a letter that I hoped would not be thrown in the wastepaper basket in anger or distress. I would not bother the addressees again if they chose not to answer, I wrote, but I would appreciate any information that they were able to give.

Some time later, in May 1986, a large brown envelope arrived from New Zealand. I opened it with a sense of excitement. I had sent copies of the letter to all six names; this was the sole response.

The sender, Githa, was the daughter-in-law of Harry, one of Eugenia's brothers, she explained. Her letter, handwritten on lined paper, was in a warm and friendly tone and she expressed no hesitation in helping me. Her children were very interested, she said, and she was sure that her husband, who had died in 1984, would have felt the same.

What knowledge she had came from another relative, Olga, the second wife of Lou, another of the Falleni brothers. Only one of the Falleni children was still alive, and he was very old. Olga herself was now elderly, but very lively still. Italian by birth, she was 'very Italian' in temperament, and was often willing to talk about the family.

According to Olga, the Falleni family had come from a small town just outside Livorno. They had left Italy in the period after the Garibaldi wars (that is, during the Risorgimento, or period of Italian unification) along with five or six other families who may have chosen to leave due to their political affiliations.

Eugenia (or Eugene, called after her maternal grandmother) was the eldest of 22 children, including two sets of twins. Seventeen of these, ten boys and seven girls, survived. The second eldest child, a girl, had been left behind as she was too young to travel when her mother followed other relatives to New Zealand. In Wellington the family lived in a series of houses in the weatherboard suburb of Newtown.

Olga had married one of the younger of Eugenia's brothers (the last child, a little girl, did not survive). Olga herself knew little about Eugenia, due to the gap of over twenty years between the eldest and youngest children. When Olga became part of the family Eugenia had already left home and the older children were not often spoken of.

Eugenia: A Man

The Falleni family around 1910. Back row, left to right: Emily, Lou, Rosie, Darky, Nita and Sonny. Middle row, seated: Eadie, parents Isola and Luigi Falleni, Lily, grandmother Eugene Buti. Seated on floor: Harry, Eadie's daughter. Photo: by permission of the Falleni family

With the letter came a photograph, a formal family portrait showing four generations of the Falleni family posed stiffly in front of a photographer's backing of ornate drapery. Before me, looking outwards with a level gaze, are the grandmother Eugene; the two Falleni parents, Isola and Luigi; four sons and five daughters; and one granddaughter. Harry Falleni, the letter-writer's father-in-law, aged ten or twelve, sits cross-legged on the floor in the left hand corner not far from a granddaughter, who looks about the same age. The other children are all young adults. The photograph was apparently taken around 1910—the time when Harry Crawford was working as a gardener and handyman at Dr Clarke's house in Wahroonga.

Luigi Falleni, Eugenia's father, seated centre right, appears as a greying, solidly built figure with receding hair and the stern expression of a man holding still for the photographer. He wears a starched collar, a three-piece suit, and a badge or decoration hangs from his watch chain. His hands rest firmly on the arms of his chair; his bearing seems to suggest patriarchal confidence.

A carrier with a horse and cart, a fisherman, a master of all trades, Luigi Falleni was known to all as a very hard man, wrote Githa.

Isola Falleni, Eugenia's mother, wears a dark, ruffled satin blouse and a severely tailored skirt; her centrally parted, dark hair is swept up in two thick wings on either side of her face. In middle age and after some 25 years of childbearing, she is also solidly built, and her only jewellery is a plain brooch, a wedding band, and what appears to be a tiny watch on a fine, waist-length chain around her neck. She gazes evenly and seriously at the world, but her broad, sensible hands are clenched a little, as if she is apprehensive of, or impatient with, the man behind the camera. Isola was a tailoress, a woman universally loved, of whom it was said that if there were a place called heaven, she would surely get there. She was described by Olga as an 'absolute delight'.

The adult sons—Sonny, Darky and Lou—are formally dressed in dark suits with the same stiff collars and watch chains as their father. The daughters—Emily, Eadie, Rosie, Nita, and Lily who is still adolescent—wear similar plain chains and pendants. Nita wears a crucifix. Two are in handsome brocaded dresses, two are in lace-collared blouses and plain long skirts. Lily, who looks as if she is trying not to smile, wears a calf-length white lace dress and white hair ribbon. Straight-backed and well-groomed, the sisters and brothers stand in a presentable group framing their parents.

Two of the sons became carriers, wrote Githa, and two were hairdressers who became very well known around Wellington. The girls, according to Olga, were 'just housekeepers'. Oddly enough—or perhaps not oddly at all—all of these children had only one or two children themselves.

The grandmother, Eugene, Isola's mother, seated on the far right, wears mourning, a little in the style of Queen Victoria, with a black lace shawl, but also a little black hat with white flowers. The close resemblance between the family members is striking. Except for the granddaughter, Eadie's daughter, who is blonde, all the children had the same dark brown hair, dark eyes and determined chins. It is not difficult to place Eugenia among them, in either her male or female guise.

When asked if the family were a happy one, Olga would say no more than, 'as happy as a big family could be, I suppose'.

Twenty-Four

WITH THE PHOTOGRAPH propped in front of me, I tried to conjure alive these figures to form the building blocks in Eugenia's personality: the hard, stern father; the gentle and long-suffering mother.

I pictured Eugenia in a weatherboard house in Coromandel Street in Newtown, a poor but decent suburb of Wellington in the final decades of the nineteenth century, in the early days after Isola's and Luigi's arrival as the still-small family struggled to find their feet in the new land. Perhaps Eugenia, watching her pregnant mother give birth year after year—while she, as eldest of the family, felt more and more a burden of responsibility as the family grew larger—became somehow imbued with an aversion to the life her mother led.

As she grew up, did she see her father and her younger brothers stride out of the house, away from the suffocating chaos of children and laundry and cooking, to other worlds and freedom, while her mother remained toiling long hours at a sewing machine? Did she watch her father, king of his household, ruling her and her sisters, as her younger brothers took their places as men beside him?

Eugenia: A Man

I wondered if it was this domineering father that Eugenia imitated in the work she did; the hard man, the jack-of-all-trades with the horse and cart. And perhaps there was something of him in the Harry Crawford who alternately bullied and cajoled his wife. Was it this man that Harry was thinking of when he told Annie Birkett that her son needed a father to guide him?

I wondered whether Eugenia knew or guessed at what passed between her mother and her father in a dim curtained bedroom in that cold windy New Zealand town; something that seemed to give her father such mysterious power over her compliant mother as the years passed and the family grew and somehow prospered. Was it this inexorable power that Eugenia might have been hoping to protect her mother and herself against by gaining the strength of a man? Or did she want to wield it herself?

IN 1874 there were 280 Italians in New Zealand; this number rose to 538 in 1878—the year after Luigi and Isola Falleni and the infant Eugenia arrived—then declined again to 397 in 1891. By the mid-1960s (unlike in Australia, where the numbers had increased quite rapidly) there were still only some 1500.

First of the known arrivals was Salvatore Cimini of Capri, master of a trading vessel, who came in the 1830s. More Italians appeared with the gold rushes, but many of these left again. Then, under Julius Vogel's government in the 1870s, came the first assisted migrants from Italy.

At this time the number of migrants to New Zealand from Germany and Scandinavia had been slowing, and

Italians, who had a high reputation in the colony as railway workers, were considered by the government as desirable replacements. John Glynn, an Englishman resident in Livorno, where he had been employed as a restaurant manager and theatrical agent, was in 1875 appointed Special Agent for Italy and charged with the responsibility of recruiting migrants.

Glynn, by means of posters and a leaflet extolling the virtues of New Zealand, by giving promises of high wages and employment in their own trades, and by accepting virtually anyone who offered, managed to recruit about 230 people. These arrived in Wellington in three main groups during 1875 and 1876. Drawn mainly from the towns, and with occupations as diverse as sculptor, locksmith, waiter, cabman, clerk, porter, telegraphist and organ grinder, the migrants were, however, disconcerted to find themselves expected to work at labouring and for less money than they had been promised. After an unsuccessful attempt to settle 53 of their number as farmers in swampy and heavily forested country at Okura, the government, disgruntled and dissatisfied with the recruits, stopped financially assisting Italian migrants, and many of the new arrivals left. Subsequent Italian settlers came in small numbers, paid their own fares, and migrated in family chains as a result of links with those already there. There followed a small aggregation of Italian market gardeners in Lower Hutt, and fishermen in Wellington, who came mainly from Massalubrense in the Bay of Naples.

Taking a narrower focus on these events, one can discover from the New Zealand archives that on 27 June 1875 an Italian woman, Eugenie [or Eugene]

Buti, aged 35, sailed from Hamburg on the German ship *Herschel* under a Captain Kauman, and reached Port Nicholson, Wellington, on 23 October of the same year. On board at the same time were some 226 passengers, mainly assisted migrants, of whom 128 were Italians, 42 were Danes, 26 were Germans, eleven were Swedes, eight were Norwegian, seven were Swiss, two were Austrian and two were from the Tyrol. Of the Italians, some were single men in their twenties who gave their occupation as farm labourer, and a proportion of the rest were skilled tradesmen. Of the 225 aboard as passengers, only 56 were adult women.

Eugene Buti was accompanying her husband Vincenzio, who gave his profession as shipwright. This was Eugene's second marriage; her previous husband, Joseph Gini, a wine merchant, had died after a mental breakdown that followed being defrauded by his business partner. With her on the *Herschel* were two children from the first marriage, Oracio, aged eleven, and Rosa, fifteen. Her other child, Isola, sixteen, with a baby of her own under a year old, had been left behind to follow on with her young husband when the child was old enough to make the long sea voyage.

Two years later, on 5 May 1877, the *Waikato*, a newly-built iron New Zealand Shipping Company clipper weighing 1000 tons, sailed from Plymouth, stopping at various ports, and reached Lyttelton, Canterbury, New Zealand on 8 August. On board, of a total of 143 passengers, 55 were English, eight were Scottish, 73 were Irish, four were Channel Islanders, and three were Italian. Most of these passengers were also assisted migrants; the majority being single English and Irish women, of whom there were 93, and who mostly gave their occupation as domestic servant. When the *Waikato* docked at Port Nicholas, Wellington, on 26 July before sailing on to Canterbury, the three Italians disembarked. These were Luigi Falleni, aged 25, who gave his profession as coachman; his wife Isola, née Gini, tailoress, aged eighteen, and their two-year-old child, born in Ardenza on 25 January 1875, called in the passenger list Eugenie. The cost of their passage was £34/14s, of which Luigi had paid £17/15s/3d just before embarkation, and of which the Butis, already in New Zealand, no doubt guaranteed the rest.

Probably unintentionally, Isola had become pregnant again in the intervening time. Their second child, Lisa, born just before their departure, was left behind with relatives.

Luigi was himself the son of Giuseppe Falleni, also a coach driver, and Asunta, née Casali: he had married Isola Gini at Livorno in 1873, when he was 22. The Ginis and the Fallenis came from the northwest coast of Italy; the region of the largely uninhabited Maremma, a salty marsh with a hinterland of small farms, vineyards, wheat fields, and steep wooded hills. In its ancient walled cities, narrow cobbled streets seek ingress among fortress-like buildings. A region of hill-top citadels: in times of threat from the outside, the traditional form of protection was a snail-like withdrawal behind stone walls.

On the coast itself lay the fortified harbour of Livorno, a busy commercial city with a famous naval academy. Among the larger ocean-going ships lining the port, which had originated from a jetty built by

Cosimo I de' Medici in 1571, were moored clusters of fishing boats that still go out after the local red mullet. The inhabitants of Livorno and its environs were no strangers to the sea.

Livorno in the early 20th century. Photo: private collection

I visited Eugenia Falleni's birthplace on a holiday in Italy in 1987. According to the telephone book in the Livorno post office, there were still Fallenis living in Ardenza, as well as Ginis, and in Livorno itself there were Butis, Ginis and Fallenis. Buti was the name of a coastal region in the area. Throughout the district, the Fallenis spread over a column of about 150 names.

From the centre of the port of Livorno, I followed the Viale Italia as it swept along the edge of the Mediterranean to the outlying town of Ardenza, where Eugenia's young parents had practised their professions of tailoress and coachman. In early autumn, when I visited, I found a windswept resort lining a flat, rocky coast, with a few small beaches. Set back from the water, ornately decorated nineteenth century holiday villas, now run down, retained an air of faded grace. There were grand hotels with imposing façades. Many of the houses had picturesque glassed-in observation towers.

I sat in the garden of a seaside coffee bar, which now, out of season, was filled with noisy groups of old men and youths, but—as was still traditional—no women. Some gypsies sat at a bare table, counting the coins they had begged. It was a cool and windy day, and the surrounding houses were closed and shuttered.

Here, over a hundred years before, Isola and Luigi might have had the opportunity to observe the manner and dress of the newly-rich middle-class industrialists and merchants who built their summer residences away from the sweltering summer heat of the inland cities. Years later, Isola may have passed on this sense of style and quality as she laboured to clothe her many children in the distant provincial city of Wellington.

AT ABOUT THE TIME Eugenia was entering her teens in Coromandel Street in Newtown, Katherine Beauchamp, later to be known as Katherine Mansfield, was born in Thorndon, at the opposite end of Wellington, to a family that had been in the Antipodes for three generations. By the time Eugenia had left her ship at Newcastle in New South Wales, nine-year-old Katherine, at school in Karori, on the city's outskirts, had had her first story accepted by a magazine called *The Lone Hand*. Katherine Mansfield later wrote in her journal of the big, white-painted square house in which she had grown up; a house with a slender, pillared verandah running around it, high on a hill and surrounded by a stone wall covered with nasturtiums. In France in 1922, just before her death at 34, she also remembered the confining suburban childhood that she too had longed to escape:

> Tinakori Road was not fashionable, it was very mixed. Of course there were some good houses in it, old ones, like ours for instance, hidden away in wildish gardens, and there was no doubt the land there would become extremely valuable, as father said, if one bought enough and hung on.
>
> It was high, it was healthy; the sun poured in the windows all day long, and once we had a decent tramway service, as Father argued ...

Katherine also noted her childhood memories of the local people: the washerwoman living next door who 'would persist in attempting to talk' to her mother over the fence, and then,

> just beyond her 'hovel', as mother called it, there lived a man who burned leather in his back yard whenever the wind blew our way. And further along there lived an endless family of halfcastes who appeared to have planted their garden with empty jam tins and old saucepans and black iron kettles without lids. And then just opposite our house there was a paling fence, and below the paling fence in a

> hollow, squeezed in almost under the fold of a
> huge gorse-covered hill, was Saunders Lane ...

Somewhere beyond Saunders Lane, in a poorer part of town, an adolescent Italian girl, dressed like a boy, was working in her grandfather's stables.

IN SEPTEMBER 1986, after various telephone conversations, another envelope arrived from New Zealand. Githa's daughter had discovered that the grandmother of a friend had known Eugenia Falleni, and her son, the friend's father, had been persuaded to write down what he remembered. This account, which was enclosed, was contained on four neatly printed pages of a small lined pad. It began, 'I can only repeat what my mother passed on to me, and what I remember.'

Eugenia was at that time nick-named 'Tally-Ho' Falleni, and as his mother, Nellie Matthews, recalled, she had a very strict father who worked her hard. The son wrote:

> When they used to walk together down
> Kent and Cambridge Terrace, instead of
> walking ladylike, Tally-Ho would jump
> over chains instead of walking around
> them, or jump over low fences anywhere.
>
> After a period of quite some time of not
> seeing her, one day someone knocked on
> grandmother's door at the bottom of Rintoul
> Street, Wellington. My mother answered
> the door to someone who was dressed as

Eugenia: A Man

a man, who asked was Mrs Matthews in.
My mother went and got her mother to
come to the door, while my mother stood
in the background so as not to be seen but
to listen to what this person had to say.

He said he had a job at Murphy's brickhill up the road, and her lodgings had been
recommended to him. My grandmother said
she was sorry, but she didn't take in board-
ers anymore. He said thank you, and left.

After he left my mother said to her mother,
'Didn't you recognise who that was? That
was Tally-Ho Falleni, dressed as a man.'

My grandmother said, 'Don't be talking stupid like that or you'll be getting yourself into trouble.'

Sometime later, the son added, Tally-Ho was taken to court for impersonating a man. Murphy, the owner of the brickhill (or brickfield) appeared and testified that she could work as well as his best worker, and he wished his other workers worked as well as she did.

The last time that she met my mother,
Tally-Ho told her that she was going to work her way as a stoker on a
ship to Australia, which she did.

After she arrived in Australia, she [or someone who wrote for her] wrote to my mother

saying she had arrived safe and that she
hardly slept at all on board ship and kept an
iron bar under her pillow for protection.

Later his mother had read of her imprisonment for murder, and he personally had read of her death after being released from jail years later.

He hoped, concluded the son, that this might be of help.

Twenty-Five

THE DAY I arrived in Wellington, in February 1987, was sunny, bright and windy. There were whitecaps on the bay and the white-painted wooden houses seemed to cling precariously to the steep, terraced hillsides as we approached the centre. The taxi man who drove me around the harbour road obviously took pleasure in his city: pointing out with some pride the prettier examples of architecture among the older wooden public buildings around the reclaimed harbour. A narrow shelf of land rimmed the deep-water port before steep, forested hills rose to encircle the city. The more modern buildings nestled in close to the water, leaving much of the urban outskirts untouched. When I ventured out walking by myself it seemed like an Australian city of twenty years ago, but pleasantly so, with rather old-fashioned displays in the shop windows, and a lack of brash advertising. A Maori boy came and asked me for money, but he said 'God bless you' when I gave it to him. In the local newspaper, which I read in a coffee shop, much of the news on the front page was English.

With Githa, who proved no less pleasant and friendly in person, I drove from the port area along Kent and Cambridge Terrace, where Eugenia had jumped over the restricting chains, to Newtown. Here the quiet weekend streets were still lined with small timber cottages, either brightly painted or white, with wooden lattice-work trimmings and corrugated iron roofs. Here was the street where two of the youngest Falleni brothers, Lou and Harry, had had their hairdressing shops; there was the wooden house where Olga had lived with her second husband. Githa took me to the Mount Victoria lookout so that I could see the layout of the city around the extraordinarily beautiful green bay. Then we drove on to Island Bay, where beyond a stone wall and a little beach of grey sand a few fishing boats were still moored: here some of the Italian families had had their fishing boats. Nothing much had changed, it seemed. It was easy to replace the few Saturday afternoon cars with horses and carts and toast-rack trams, and mentally weed out the modern buildings to leave the sleepy streets as they had been a hundred years before. In 1900, Wellington had been a predominantly Anglo-Saxon town of 34,000 people, with a few Chinese shopkeepers and sailors of an assortment of nationalities from the visiting ships—along with a few smugglers—and its supporting industries were timber and wood. It was still a quiet town.

Olga soon finished the story she had started to tell. Her tiny, immaculate living room was decorated with glass vases of brightly coloured silk flowers, tapestry cushion covers and tinted photographs of her family. She shrugged at my initial attempts to skirt delicately around certain subjects: what happened, happened, no one could change that, she said. I put the little tape recorder on the floor between us.

Eugenia: A Man

The Falleni family came from Ardenza, near Livorno, a small town. That's where Eugenia was born. She was the oldest. Then they had another little girl, Lisa, and this one they left in Italy when they got on the boat, because at this time it took three or four months to come to New Zealand by sail. She was too small, the voyage was too long. The mother left her with the father-in-law's sisters, two sisters who had never married, and they looked after the little girl. And at a later time when they sent for her and said would she like to come to New Zealand she said no, because by this time she knew the sisters like her mother. I don't know what that family did in Italy. In Italy they were not rich and not poor, I think.

So Eugenia was the eldest. Lisa was the one in Italy. I wrote to the aunts a few times after the war, because they found me through the consul. We sent some parcels, but after that nobody answered. Now I don't know where they are.

They came to Wellington, the Fallenis, because lots of people from the Livorno region came to Wellington. In the first boat there were four or five families, five or six families. But Mr and Mrs Falleni stayed up the line, at Wanganui, for a while. The old lady, Mrs Falleni, I remember her telling me that the Maoris would trade anything for a bar of soap in those days. They would eat it like cheese.

Mrs Falleni's mother—Eugenie, Mrs Buti—had come here before, with her second husband. Mrs Falleni's father had the name Gini, he was well-to-do, he was a wine and spirit merchant, but then he died and her mother married again to Mr Buti, and they came to New Zealand with her two children. These were Rosina and Oracio. But Isola, the other, was already married to Luigi Falleni, and so she was left behind and they came later. So Mrs Buti had three children, but all with Gini, none with Buti.

I don't know why they left Italy. Sometimes I was talking about it to Mrs Falleni, but I could see that she would rather not say anything.

I don't know what the early years were like for them, but after, when I met them, they seemed to be a very good pair. They went through a very poor time. He would go out fishing; she was a very good tailoress, she worked hard. She lived a good life and looked after her family. Saturday and Sunday, she would use the two days to do all the washing and ironing and mending the clothes for all the kids. When she died, the Monsignor Carey said, if this woman does not go to Paradise, nobody will. The old man, Mr Falleni, he died first. The old lady did not want to live after he died, so she died too, seventeen days later.

Mr Falleni, he was fishing up in Wanganui,

Eugenia: A Man

and then he came to Wellington and got
a carrier, a horse and cart. Furniture he'd
carry, fruit and vegetables from the markets
and things to the shops. Then the two sons
did the same, Sonny and Darky. Two of the
daughters became tailoresses, Eadie and Emily.
And two were hairdressers, Lou and Harry.

Mr and Mrs Falleni were very good
to me. When you get old you forget to be hard. But in his young days
he was a hard man, Mr Falleni.

I can tell you what I heard from someone
else's mouth. People who knew the family,
they blamed not the father for what happened
to Eugenia, but the grandmother's husband—
Buti. At this time he had a stable. And Eugenia
was always working there among the men.
So this is why she grew up to be like a man,
because when she was small she was always
working there. All the children went to school,
but Eugenia would run away from school.

I came to Wellington in 1926, I didn't know
the Falleni family until a couple of years after
that. We lived somewhere else, then we went
to live in Newtown, and then I met the old
lady. They were living in Riddiford Street
then. They moved, but not a lot. They used
to live all around the Newtown area. But we
used to live in Adelaide Road near the Post
Office. I met Mrs Falleni one day inside the

Post Office, because I couldn't speak English very well, and she said, 'I can help you.'

None of the children were living at home at that time. She was quite old then. But when my husband separated from his first wife he went back to stay with his mother. When I met them I was a widow of 24. My husband had died of TB a couple of years before, and I went out to work cleaning houses. I had children, you see, and I couldn't get a pension at that time because I wasn't naturalised. After a time my husband came to my house as a boarder, and we married after a while.

My husband was a long way down in the family. There was Eugenia, then Lisa, then Eadie, then Rosie, then Annie, then Darky… My husband said he didn't remember anything about Eugenia, all he remembered was her playing the tambourine in the Salvation Army Band when he was a child, but just like it was in a dream. He remembered her as a wonderful-looking woman, but as if in a dream. He said she looked a little like Eadie. Everyone said she was a beautiful woman.

She was a beautiful woman who wanted to be a man and who dressed like a man. She went down to the west coast. She drove four dangerous horses, she was the best coachman of all. She loved riding horses; she was a better horseman than any of the men.

Eugenia: A Man

She worked in the brickworks as a man, she dressed herself as a man in the morning and in the evening she went home and dressed as a woman. Only Rosie and Emily knew—Aunt Rosie and Aunt Emily, two of the older ones. They would go on the same train at night, Rosie and Emily, and she would say, if you tell Dad, you know what will happen to you. So she would dress again in women's clothing before she went inside. She would drive a horse and cart down the west coast and work as a bricklayer in Miramar—it's a hard job. She must have been a good actress, very clever, to do this.

And then she went away. She was about twenty then, I think. With this captain on the boat, so they said. And got married to him. The old lady said this, but this is what she had been told. It might not have been true.

When Eugenia went away to Australia she wanted to come back, but they stopped her from coming back. When the father and the mother found out about all this they got such a shock they tried everything to stop her coming back. She had never done any terrible thing, but there was the name, the family name: So they stopped her. And then after all this these other things happened, with this woman.

I know how the old lady felt. She did not

want to talk about it. She was a very clean-living woman, and she did not want to have anything wrong in the family. But I think, with so many children, there would have to be a black sheep, anyway. The others all turned out very good, and married good, and were hardworking. But there would have to be one.

My husband, he told me a little bit here and there, but no one else in the family told me anything, not Nita, not Rosie. The old lady, a couple of times she came to me when she got this paper from Australia, but I could tell she did not want to say anything.

The old lady nearly passed away when it all happened. She did not want trouble. She always said, if Eugenia had married this captain, when she went to the court, why couldn't she have used his name? And not bring the family into it?

I knew how she felt, even though she did not want to talk about it. When the paper came and said Eugenia had died, she was relieved, because before you'd never know when she would come back, and cause all these problems. She was very sad, but she was also relieved. Because now it was all over.

I don't know. Everyone said she was a really beautiful woman. One man from Auckland wanted to marry her. He's dead now, too.

Eugenia: A Man

He had a good job in the Parliament House, and later he bought a beautiful hotel in Auckland. Her mother, Mrs Falleni, said to Eugenia, why don't you marry him? He's a nice man for you, he will look after you.

Eugenia said, 'If you want him to marry, why don't you marry him yourself?' She said this to her mother! And I met the man afterwards. He said he did everything he could to marry her. He said to her mother, 'Don't you worry, I will marry her and calm her down.' But no, she did not want to marry anyone. I don't think she needed men, Eugenia.

And then she left.

Back in my hotel room, I thought of the notes I had previously written about Eugenia. One of the effects of reading the court records and newspaper stories had been to create in me a great unwillingness to project onto her any more than had already been projected— by a public prosecutor who needed a motive, by tabloid journalists who needed to titillate a jaded reader, by a doctor whose observations even when sympathetic were hampered by a lack of modern knowledge. I had been determined to consider the sources and to extract from them only what might have been objectively true. How Eugenia might have thought and felt herself was something that no one could venture to say.

And yet it had been impossible not to speculate: I had already found myself writing that Eugenia had arrived in Sydney from Newcastle 'harbouring the terrifying knowledge' that she was pregnant. But the Eugenia who had just now been sketched for me by the old woman might equally well have been angry. The nearest I had been able to approach the young Eugenia was an image in the romantic memory of a young boy, passed on many years later as a grown man to his second wife. He had thought her beautiful, and family legend had it that she was strong and spirited.

So now I tried to picture Eugenia leaving her home, leaving behind this eligible and persistent suitor, perhaps after having been publicly exposed in a Wellington court, turning her eyes to the sailing ships that came and went in the busy port, and waiting for the opportunity to make her move.

I wondered how Eugenia must have felt as she worked among the men at the brickyard and later the sailors on board ship, wanting to be a man, outwardly being one, yet repelled by male attention when it was directed at her; how she would have coped with the loneliness, after leaving behind the intimacy and gossip of a volatile Italian family, and the confidences shared with her sisters Rosie and Emily. Now it was no longer possible to slip back into the guise of femininity, to put on the skirts and high-heeled boots that allowed her access back to the familiar routine of the weatherboard house in Newtown, the shared meals and work, and the games of the younger children under the grandmotherly eyes of Eugene—even if such comfort was ambivalently received. Eugenia was like the eldest princess in the story who escapes to an underground kingdom and wears out pair after pair of dancing shoes in the court of the fairy princes, before retreating to her own bed at dawn, with only the worn out shoes as evidence to confound her parents. Had it been an adventure in the beginning? Now, with return impossible, ahead of Eugenia there was only the rough male world, the danger, the loneliness of the outsider, and the eternal vigilance necessary so that no observer would discover her secret. Her beauty and strength of spirit would have faced a rough test in shipboard life and in the near destitution on the edge of turn-of-the-century Australian society.

I tried to place Eugenia, a slim youth in a workman's cap, in the noisy, casual ambience of a Sydney hotel, manhandling the metal barrels of beer down wooden ramps from the brewers' carts to be stacked in the cellar before broaching. Washing hundreds of glasses, swabbing the tiled floors of an inner city bar to rid them of the smell of stale beer and vomit, perhaps helping the publican to eject the odd drunk or troublemaker. I wondered if young Harry Crawford moved easily and unnoticed among the noisy drinkers trying to down their ration before closing time in the 'six o'clock swill'—a world where no other women safely ventured except the barmaids, and they protected both by the bar and by the age-old conventions of barmaiding.

And I wondered what must have gone through Harry's mind as he walked through the saloon bar, the dark hole of pseudo-respectability where the outcast women sat to drink their beer-and-lemonade shandies and wait for their husbands, or nurse their alcoholism and knitting in a nicely segregated purdah, shunned by the genteel. The saloon bar, even now, was in most cases a sad place, a refuge for failed domesticity; the public bar, even if a haven of male solidarity and camaraderie, was, in the last analysis, also often a place of failure, a place for seeking oblivion and the avoidance of wives. As young Harry Crawford replaced the metal baskets of dirty glasses with clean ones and wiped down the counters, did he keep his eyes down and avoid conversation, drink a little whisky and then a little more? The prospect of a cheap room, boarding house food, and solitude for the rest of his life must at times have seemed insupportable.

I tried to place Harry Crawford in his job at the slaughterhouse, during his three long years at the National Meatworks at Balmain—the hot blood sluicing down the concrete gutters; the give of supple hide, still warm from life, laid open by steel knives; the jarring grind of saws through shank bones; the ever-present smell of blood in his nose as the skins were punched from the flesh and the cavernous insides disgorged the endless, greenish stomachs, intestines, livers and spleens; the kidneys being cut from their encasings of fat; and the skull axed open like a faggot of wood to pluck out the brain and the tongue. Harry Crawford in cotton cap, gumboots and a long apron, striding among the men who tendered the bawling cattle to the hammer, to the straining metal hooks that elevated them, clanging, one after the other, and then swilling the buckets of water that washed away the rivers of blood from the wet floors.

And later, when he lost a finger in one of the meat packing machines, I wondered whether he bandaged it himself, waited for it to heal, and then continued on—a little tougher, a little harder, a little less respectful of pain and mortality, than many men are ever expected to be.

Twenty-Six

EUGENIA'S period at sea—which might have offered some of the most important clues to her later actions—still contained the most mystery, and (seemingly) encouraged the most invention.

James Holledge, writing in the *Daily Mirror* on 3 October 1955, stated that, after running away to sea, 'for some years' Eugenia:

> adventured around the Pacific on a variety of vessels. She lived the foc's'le life with the rest of the crew and preserved her secret without trouble.
>
> She roistered around island ports such as Suva, Papeete and Honolulu and was ready to swing a punch or down a grog with the best.

This story is illustrated with a clear photograph of Eugenia that indeed shows her as a beauty—she appears as a sensitive-faced young man with milky skin and short, smooth-brushed hair, gazing straight at the camera. Her features—strong for a woman, but even—already show a hint of melancholy. The original of this head and shoulders photograph, in the News Ltd picture files, proved to be a postcard portrait supplied by H. M. Ashby and Co. of Sydney, which Eugenia herself (although the picture was obviously taken earlier) had mailed in 1915.

Written in immature copperplate in indelible pencil, no doubt by someone else, it is addressed to 'Dear George' and signed 'with love from H. Crawford'. 'I am sending you my photo for [a] keepsake' says the brief message, after expressing a hope that George has enjoyed his trip. (This could be George Parnell, son of Lydia Parnell, both of whom would later give evidence at Eugenia's trial.) The handsome youth, Harry Crawford, on the other side of the card is wearing a well cut three-piece suit with a carnation in the buttonhole, a broad striped tie and a high, stiff collar.

Eugenia: A Man

Eugenia as a young man, from a photographic postcard taken in Sydney between 1900 and 1915. 'I am sending you my photo for [a] keepsake' someone had written on the back at Eugenia's direction, 'with love from H. Crawford'. Photo: News Limited

A version of the story printed in the *Sun* of 13 December 1958 maintained that Eugenia had signed up at sixteen as a cabin boy on a Norwegian barque that was trading from New Zealand among the Pacific Islands. Even in the cramped quarters of the windjammer's forecastle, the writer claims, Eugenia was able to maintain her deception for 'nearly six years'. Her undoing was an Italian seaman called 'Martello', who in their conversations together in Italian apparently gained enough clues to guess her secret. According to this source also, Eugenia left the barque in 1899, pregnant to Martello, whom she never saw again.

On 10 September 1967 Holledge, in a series in the *Sunday Mirror* entitled 'Wild Men and Women of

Sydney', expanded his previous account to describe the 'dark-eyed, vivacious teenage Italian' who adventured around the South Seas. 'Years later, when the story of Eugene Falleni made front page news, former shipmates who remembered her name came forward', he wrote.

>Old salts recalled roistering around Suva,
>Papeete and Honolulu with Harry Crawford.
>
>'He was a bit wild and boisterous,' one
>of them told a New Zealand newspaper.
>'You know what young fellows are like.
>
>'But he was a good mate to have behind
>you in a tight corner. He could swing a
>punch and down a grog with the best.'
>
>Then Eugene Falleni shipped aboard an Italian vessel. The captain could talk to her in the native tongue she used in her parents' home and before long he had discovered the secret of the hard-drinking and hard-swearing sailor.

I could find no evidence that any of this was true. The New Zealand newspapers around the dates of Eugenia's committal and trial did not incorporate any of this latter material. The main body of evidence pointed to Eugenia being around twenty when she went to sea, and to her remaining on board a much shorter time. As for 'Martello', allegedly the captain of the ship on which Eugenia left Wellington, the New Zealand papers—obviously finding no sea captain of this name in the local shipping lists—qualified the story of their alleged marriage with 'according to what Falleni told the police'. Others leaned towards the version that Eugenia thus must have grown up in Italy and married Martello there. Like them, I could find no evidence that 'Martello' had ever existed, at least under that name, on land or at sea.

But whatever Falleni's initial relationship with Josephine's father, and whatever his identity, it seems unlikely that there was ever a 'sentimental attachment', much less a marriage, between them. The stronger likelihood was that Eugenia was sexually assaulted, or taken advantage of, or otherwise somehow coerced by him.

Eugenia's initial motivation for leaving New Zealand was probably to escape a small society that had discovered her double life, and to leave with a ship, either passing as a male crew member or under the protection of one, was an expedient way of doing so. A liaison with a crew member, even if initially entered into voluntarily, may have degenerated into sexual exploitation by force or blackmail once on board.

However, if Eugenia was indeed passing as a young boy, the successful deception would not necessarily be a safeguard against sexual molestation. Presumably it was Eugenia herself who was the source of the story of 'violent usage' cited by Moran, and perhaps at a time (long after the trial?) when there was no further reason to lie. 'It is said,' wrote Moran, 'that the captain, having surprised the secret of her sex, used her violently and then abandoned her in her pregnancy.' Almost certainly, as Moran himself suggests, if Eugenia was raped or otherwise exploited at a young age, she felt humiliated and traumatised by the experience.

As to her attacker's station, it seemed just as likely that he was merely a seaman who discovered her secret some time into the voyage. The story of the marriage, and 'Martello's' status as captain, Eugenia no doubt invented to shield her family and Josephine, and the same probably applies to her attempt to adopt his name. In addition—and aside from needing to cater to contemporary morality—she had been got the better of by a man, which must have shamed her. None of her actions before or after the birth of Josephine point to a prior satisfying physical relationship with a man.

In later life Eugenia would appear, on the evidence available, to have avoided much close emotional contact with men. Perhaps she knew from experience that her male workmates could not be allowed to know her too well. Perhaps she knew that, away from the distractions of work, in the life of the pubs and two-up games, they might soon begin to find Harry Crawford 'odd'.

The fact that Eugenia chose to work among men, and to 'be' one, was clearly not out of a desire for male company. At a time when in Australian society it would have seemed more 'natural' for her to fulfil the traditions of male friendship, or mateship, she generally steered clear of other men, or they of her. Odd exceptions occur, usually where they might be of some use to her (Moran), or were much younger: the boy George Parnell, and the young man mentioned by Harry Birkett, who took Crawford and himself to Mrs

Schieblich's house. But for friends, companions and confidantes, she chose women.

And of the women Eugenia knew well, most apparently showed a ready acceptance of her. None among them seems to have discovered her secret unless she was told. Like a cuckoo in the nest, she relied on the nurturing instincts of other women (which she herself lacked) to look after her daughter and her stepson, usually without adequate payment. On the evidence, she was domestically impractical, unwilling even to cook herself breakfast. For practical support, she passed among a wide-ranging network of women, landladies and neighbours, coming back to them repeatedly, maintaining the contact by occasional visits, relying on them for shelter and human warmth.

Of the witnesses at the trial who had had close personal relations with Eugenia, all were women (with the exception of Harry Birkett). Her male neighbours were peripheral to her life. It was women who knew her best and who were most attached to her. Harry Crawford was a man not because he liked men, it would seem, but because he wanted and needed the company of women.

ALTHOUGH initially I could find no record of Eugenia's previous encounter with the courts in Wellington, this was also intriguing. The incident shed new light on some of her later actions, particularly on her incriminating behaviour after her arrest, and her obvious previous fear of the police, mentioned by Josephine in her statement.

It also went a long way towards explaining Eugenia's damning remark to Robson, 'I suppose now I will have to go to gaol,' not long after she was taken to the Central Police Station for questioning. If Eugenia had been charged with little more than impersonating a man in New Zealand, she no doubt believed that this was a crime.

Unfortunately, however, it also provides her with a possible motive for wishing to be rid of Annie Birkett, slightly different in emphasis from the prosecution's. If Moran were right and Annie intended to seek an annulment of her marriage, Eugenia may have believed that this revelation of her secret in official quarters would be sufficient to have her arrested again. If Annie had not finally made up her mind to take action until eight months after her discovery, this may be what precipitated the events of the Eight Hour Day weekend in 1917.

Eugenia probably believed from the beginning that she was guilty, if not of murder, at least of a crime for which she could be imprisoned. It also provides her with a strong motive for leaving New Zealand: after such a public humiliation and family scandal, she was no doubt more than ready to run away.

I found myself wondering again about her automatic rejection (though no doubt prompted by her counsel) of 'bearded, old or grey-haired' men from the jury that tried her. An obvious explanation was that she did not wish to be judged by men who reminded her of her strict father, although her father, while bearded and grey-haired in later life, would have been only in his early forties when Eugenia left home. Perhaps that rejection owed more to a memory of a long-ago appearance before a judge at a Wellington courthouse.

How many more of the damning revelations of

her trial might have other explanations when put in another context: the gun, which became an indicator of violent intentions when found by the police, was probably a sensible precaution for a woman, already once violated, who was working and living in the rough milieu of hotels and meatworks.

Twenty-Seven

MORAN, commenting on Eugenia's personality, wrote:

> Obviously, this was a woman with the mental capacity of some lower animal. She had none of the brilliant attainments of so many perverts. Nor was she aggressively masculine. There was nothing of the bearded woman about her. She had no religious sentiments of any kind, and not the slightest evidence of any spirituality. She was just a half-wild creature who felt herself apart and different, who had grown cunning and furtive, hiding her secret and satisfying her needs. She must have long since learned how the common people hated the habit she practised. She must have gone always harnessed with fear. It is only by the light of that ever-present fear we can hope to understand her problem and her crime …
>
> For Eugenia Falleni was a homosexualist … She had murdered the woman whom she married—the word of course is inexact—and who had at

> last become aware of her guilty secret. A panic
> of fear had then invaded her. She became like
> a creature which cornered, turns savage claws
> on the pursuer. Society had been hunting her
> all these furtive years. Society had been perse-
> cuting her—she was not conscious of any real
> wrong-doing. It was those others who were
> at fault; they it was who were all out of step.

Moran, in his analysis of Eugenia, concludes that she was of low intelligence. He disregards the fact that, by the time of her trial, Eugenia seems to have maintained with some consistency at least five variations of her identity (although several of them may have been little more than aliases). The complexity of her life appears to have escaped him.

Firstly, there was her 'real' or birth identity as Eugenia (that is, Eugene, Eugenie, Nina or Lena) Falleni, as she was known to her family in New Zealand, to her daughter Josephine and Mrs De Angelis, and perhaps to a few others in Australia. This identity, in later life most secret, was primarily that of an Italian woman, a daughter and a mother herself. In time this transmogrified to 'Nina', or 'Tally-Ho', the Italian-speaking girl who dressed as a boy. This identity, developed out of her impersonations of a boy in New Zealand, was revealed in Australia only to the Italian Marcellina Bombelli and her family, although doubtless others knew of it. (Signora Bombelli had been 'told' that Falleni was a woman, she said.)

Then there was Eugenia, or Eugene, Martello, an alias mentioned in police reports, although there is little direct evidence of her using it, except in claiming to police that she had been married to a man called Martello.

There was 'Jack' Crawford, a variation of Harry Crawford, who was Henrietta Schieblich's tenant. Jack Crawford was known by a woman who was herself an outcast: an enemy alien and the wife of an enemy alien in a prison camp for the duration of the war.

Finally there was Harry Leo (or Leon) Crawford, Eugenia's most consistent male identity, an identity so complete that it convinced two women in turn, with both of whom Crawford lived in marital domesticity. In the second instance, Harry Crawford became a Scotsman from Edinburgh—possibly a concession to his wife's origins—and a 'mechanical engineer' by trade. Harry Crawford would, if he could, be what other people most needed him to be.

A number of factors aided these deceptions. This was a time when male and female modes of dress were strictly differentiated: a working man's clothes were usually in drab colours, consisting of loose trousers and square-cut jacket, and always a hat or cap worn out of doors. A woman's clothes at the turn of the century accentuated waist and breasts: skirts were mandatory, hair was long and worn up, delicate gloves and elaborate hats were customary. The visual cues that distinguished men from women were much less ambiguous than in modern times. In addition, Eugenia apparently had modified her walk, swinging her arms from the shoulders and striding out in a jerky way that she saw as masculine. She cropped her hair, used rough language, smoked cigars and drank whisky, which further distanced her from accepted norms of womanly behaviour. At a time when transvestism was not a matter of common knowledge, and 'transsexualism' or 'transgender' words not yet coined, the world saw what it expected to see. Then there was Jean Falleni, prisoner of Long Bay, and finally Jean Ford.

The changes in name parallel a slide in identity: the tomboy child who becomes an androgynous youth who runs away to sea and, unwillingly, bears a child. The young drifter who becomes a grown man, a workman. The married man who becomes a female lag, who in turn becomes a respectable old woman. The period in which Eugenia lived in a male identity eventually totalled over 25 years.

In the process Eugenia lost and regained her nationality as well as her sex. An Italian woman, she became nominally an Australian man. Under her own name in prison, she would finally, in old age, live as a female and again adopt an Anglo-Saxon name.

Throughout this process, Eugenia seems to have had a naïve conviction that people would accept whatever she told them—a conviction bolstered by the fact that, on the whole, they did.

Probably it was partly this mistaken sense of security that led to the fatal contradictions and carelessness in the initial versions of events she produced for her neighbours to cover the disappearance of Annie Birkett. It was only with this occurrence that Harry Crawford's patched-together life started to unravel.

But if I had been looking for a wronged woman, a heroine unjustly accused, I had not found her. All I had found was a sad and complicated story.

Twenty-Eight

WHETHER Eugenia had the nature of a violent killer is debatable.

The precise movements of Harry Crawford over the few days in late September 1917 during which Annie Birkett died did not become altogether clear during the trial. Neither did the events leading up to that death.

Neighbours saw Annie and Harry setting out from home on Friday 28 September. The testimony concerning the woman seen wandering in the bush in the previous week, who was wearing similar clothes and also carrying a suitcase (of bamboo rather than cardboard), seems to have been a red herring. This woman may or may not have been the woman later 'located' by the police, but it is unlikely that she was the woman whose body was found. Despite the defence's attempt to cast doubt on this, the major body of evidence indicates that the body was Annie Birkett's. The only remaining mystery concerned the exact circumstances in which she died.

Somehow, after Annie at least had eaten a meal of chicken, and one or both of the party had drunk from a flagon of whisky, Annie was burned, possibly alive, either by accident or intent. The lack of signs of a struggle suggests that she was not conscious at the time. The prosecution suggested that Harry had struck her, although the evidence of violence was far from conclusive. At what point between Friday and Monday these alleged events occurred was not entirely clear.

The bottle containing remnants of kerosene, found the day after the discovery of the body, was certainly incriminating, and could seem to indicate either premeditation or guilt—if it had been proven that it was connected with the case. In the three years between the discovery of the body and the trial, the bottle had migrated from 'about six yards from where the fire had been burning' (*Sun*, 4 October 1917), to 'about five or six feet from the body' (Sergeant Gorman in his evidence to the court, 18 August 1920).

And if Harry murdered Annie in cold blood, as the case for the prosecution implied, and then burned her, he was definitely not thinking clearly after the act. He did not wait to make sure the body was completely consumed, and he did not go back to remove any of the evidence—suitcase, jewellery, utensils—that could assist in identifying the body and linking him to the crime.

Instead, he seems to have returned to wander in the area for two or three days, apparently grieving—or at least in a state of trauma, shock, confusion, or alcoholic withdrawal—while going home to sleep on at least one of the nights, Saturday. On the others he may have slept in the bush. He made no effort to hide from passers-by. The evidence suggesting when he might have killed Annie or burned her unconscious body was conflicting: the food in the stomach suggesting Friday (if Annie were alive when burned), the sightings of a fire by some witnesses suggesting late afternoon on Monday.

But whatever had happened in the intervening time, by the evening of Monday 1 October, Harry Crawford had pulled himself together sufficiently to return to Drummoyne and begin spreading the story among the neighbours that Annie had left him. In the space of a week he had organised the sale of the household furniture and some of her possessions, and made arrangements to leave the district.

Yet his actions still showed a naïve despair at both his and Annie's fates. Soon after the finding of the body, and sufficiently distraught as to be talking to himself, he questioned both Harry Birkett and George Parnell about the newspaper stories, seemingly unconscious of the fact that he was incriminating himself. If this represented an effort to find out if he was to be a murder suspect, it was badly miscalculated.

Now his actions became even more erratic.

According to Moran's account of the events, apparently confirmed by Harry Birkett's deposition and Mrs Schieblich's evidence at the Police Court, Harry Crawford undertook what may have been a second murder attempt. He took the fourteen-year-old Harry Birkett to Watson's Bay, and on the high cliffs of The Gap, tried for some three quarters of an hour to lure him to the edge. They should throw stones into the waves, he said. But the boy was afraid, intimidated by Crawford's sullen and silent mood. According to the statement Harry Birkett made when he first went to the police:

Eugenia: A Man

> He walked out and up near the lighthouse
> and down near a little park and all over
> the place, generally speaking he was roam-
> ing about and would not speak to me. I
> had been asking him questions, where he
> was going and why he was going here
> and there and other questions, but mostly
> he did not reply, so I gave up asking.

The pair returned to Circular Quay by ferry and then walked through the Domain and Botanical Gardens, where they sat down close to the gates and Birkett ate the cakes he had got from Sargeants. 'We were there for a couple of hours, during which time he never spoke and appeared to be deep in thought,' reported Birkett.

A second attempt at Bellevue Hill also resulted in Harry Crawford losing his impulse to act. After helping to dig two different holes in a deserted area on a night so rainy that no one would have come across them by accident, Birkett said, 'I was following Crawford. I always walked behind him. I was somehow afraid to walk near him.'

Harry Birkett was suspicious, he told the police. Crawford would not tell him why he wanted the hole, so Birkett kept an eye on him all the time. 'When I got tired, he dug some more. Then he got out and walked away. As he walked in and out of the bushes, turning from one place to another, I kept right behind him.'

After the second hole was dug, and either having failed to strike or not having an opportunity due to Harry Birkett's watchfulness, Harry Crawford took the frightened and wet boy home.

After this episode, said Birkett, he continued to go to work as usual. Some days later he became ill, and Crawford took him to Signora Bombelli's at 156 Cathedral Street, blaming the food at Mrs Schieblich's. Here Birkett lived mainly by himself. Crawford came occasionally to talk to his landlady, but did not have much to do with the boy. In March 1919 Birkett left Mrs Bombelli's for her son Frank's place at Sans Souci.

Harry Crawford, meanwhile, went on to a succession of jobs, and—according to some newspaper accounts—deteriorated in manner and appearance, continued to drink heavily, and lost job after job due to erratic behaviour. In time he began to court another woman; a woman he would later describe as his only friend in Australia, and whom he would want to protect from the events of his past. He spruced himself up, bought new clothes and cut down on his drinking, said the newspapers. He married Elizabeth King Allison at the Canterbury registry in 1919, and lived with her at Stanmore while working at an Annandale hotel.

For two years and nine months young Harry Birkett was apparently too preoccupied with the business of survival to do much about his mother's disappearance. He wrote to old neighbours to see if they had news of her, and eventually he tracked down his aunt. Meanwhile, he must have pondered the things he knew and guessed at.

When finally he went to the police on 13 June 1920, Harry Birkett told them that he had last seen Harry Crawford eight or nine months before at Richardson's Hotel. Frank Bombelli had told him that Harry was working there, so he went to ask if he had heard anything of his mother.

When Crawford saw the boy he asked him how he was getting on and where he was working. Birkett told him, and Crawford said he was too busy to speak to him then as it was so near to six o'clock (closing time), but asked him to call by next day. Birkett called the next day as arranged, but by this time Crawford had already left the hotel, and Birkett had not seen him since.

THE CURRENT LITERATURE of female-to-male transsexualism suggested that in many cases when it occurs there was a dominant father, a submissive mother, and a deep-seated belief that the female condition was disadvantageous and dangerous.

A cluster of common characteristics noted by clinical psychologists included that the associated behaviour began early in childhood, with cross-dressing occurring before puberty and tomboy behaviour evident in adolescence. There might be a protective attitude towards other women, and a dissociation from the father, who was also imitated. The adopted sex role might be stereotyped, even caricatured. The subject might be domineering towards women. This last might include an active and domineering part in sexual relations (in which, however, the partner was not generally permitted to make contact with the genitals). Libido was often quite low. Subjects could display impulsive, often criminal behaviour, and might be alcoholic. The subject could be aggressive, and most exhibited depression. Often, they were diagnosed as impulsive, with sociopathic tendencies.

In a loose interpretation, Eugenia's experience could

be made to fit this pattern. Following one line of speculation, one could argue that Eugenia, observing her mother year in and year out giving birth to babies that either lived or died (seventeen survivals from 22 births), might have been profoundly affected by it. The births would probably have occurred at home and the older daughters might well have been expected to aid the midwife. This female role—menial, ill-educated, and victim to the reproductive cycle, which in Eugenia's mother resulted in the development of saintlike attributes—was one that Eugenia chose to discard. When later she fell victim to pregnancy herself, she rapidly rejected laundering clothes (her mother's and sisters' role) in favour of driving a horse and cart (her father's). Following a different line of speculation, it is possible that, coming from a family of unusually numerous children, Eugenia was influenced by a desire to compete with her father and possibly her brothers for her mother's attention and affection, and to do this successfully she might have believed she would need to be male. Following the clues of her family history, one could conjecture that Eugenia herself felt unwanted—the female child who had initially prevented her young mother from accompanying the rest of her family to the Antipodes.

And then her own birth was followed rapidly by another pregnancy, another daughter—but this one easily discarded, left behind with relatives. (Would they, I wondered, so easily have left behind a son?) And then again, in the years after arriving in New Zealand, two more daughters followed. In this traditional Italian family, was the arrival of the fifth child—at last a son—greeted in some way that confirmed to Eugenia, a little girl now between six and eight years old, the comparative worthlessness of daughters? Was this mirrored in Eugenia's treatment of her own unwanted, but never completely abandoned, daughter? And in her subsequent life with women, was it this basic need for love and affirmation that Eugenia was attempting to fulfil? It might have been the threat of rejection, rather than of exposure, on Annie Birkett's discovery of her sex, that led to an emotional breakdown and Annie's subsequent death.

Although a psychologist might argue that Eugenia exhibited some of the classic symptoms of what would now be termed sociopathy—her childhood attempts to run away from school and home; her later inability to remain in one job or maintain longstanding relationships; her tendency to lie; her drinking and abusive behaviour; and her apparent destructiveness of other people's property—one has to consider that all this behaviour might equally validly have resulted from the strain of having to live the way she did. Although a psychologist might further include in this diagnosis a capability to commit murder without remorse, Eugenia does not appear to have had the nature of a conscienceless killer.

The patterns in Eugenia's life would seem to indicate that, if Eugenia—or Harry Crawford—did kill Annie Birkett, she herself might not have known the real reason for what she did. Her impulse towards violence was awakened—though in most instances inhibited by a failure of will—only in very specific circumstances.

One could argue that these occurred only when someone stood in the way of Eugenia being a man.

The first instance of expressed hostility was towards

the child Josephine, if Mrs De Angelis can be taken as a reliable witness. What more painful proof of Eugenia's own femaleness than a child, conceived unwillingly, and probably through sexual assault? Josephine was incontrovertible evidence that Eugenia was a woman, and could be treated by a man as women have been treated throughout history.

The second instance was towards the major witness to her concealed female nature, her 'wife'—now, at worst, actively threatening to expose her to the authorities, and at best a mute but constant reminder that someone else possessed this damning knowledge. Perhaps, merely because she now knew, Annie Birkett became an object of fear and repulsion as much as of love. Other people knew, admittedly, but none in the intolerable position of being also her lover.

The third instance was towards the person of Harry Birkett, thirteen-year-old witness to the events surrounding Annie's disappearance. Although Birkett represented a concrete danger—how much did he know and guess?—Falleni does not seem to have been unduly concerned at the chances of detection. She told an inconsistent story and seemed to expect people to believe it. Why not young Harry too? The actual threat he presented seems out of proportion to her dislike and fear of him. One suspects that it was his intimate connection with Annie, and the painful reminder of what Annie represented, that was more important.

Whatever reasons Harry Crawford might have tried to find to justify his violent impulses towards these three people—and whatever practical reasons he may have had for wishing to be rid of them—the fact remains that these three people were the living reminders of Harry Crawford's femaleness.

EX-POLICEMAN Harry Cox in his series 'My Strangest Murder Cases', No 3 of which, 'The Man-Woman Killer', appeared in the *Sun-Herald* of 11 June 1961, maintains that Falleni battered Annie to death as she was about to open the picnic basket and burned her body on a pyre of logs, described as 'a huge bonfire'. He goes on to say that when he saw her in Long Bay before her release and asked her about her motivation for the crime, all he could get from her was that 'she had to do it'—a remark that suggests that by this time Eugenia had given up maintaining her innocence.

Harry Cox further claims that Eugenia's baby survived her attempt (or attempts) to smother it, and further that she 'often got drunk, staggered into the Italian woman's house, demanded the return of Josephine, and when this was refused bashed into both of them with her fists'. However, his account is in so many other details inaccurate that the basis of this allegation is unclear. None of this information emerged in the course of the trial. What does emerge, however, is an image of an unhappy person, able neither to return to her own family nor to completely let go of the baby about which she felt so ambivalent.

The true extent of Eugenia's capacity for physical violence is hard to pin down. Harry's other traditionally 'male' characteristics were unpleasant ones: heavy drinking, bad language and verbal abuse of his wife, Annie Birkett. However, none of the witnesses at the trial, though attesting to violent rows, seemed ever to have seen Harry physically abuse

Annie. If Harry Birkett had ever seen Crawford strike or otherwise ill-treat his mother, or had observed her to be bruised or crying; surely he would not have forgotten it and would have mentioned it later in his deposition. It is arguable that Harry Crawford's references to giving his wife 'a jolly good crack' were just Harry adopting a 'manly' posture. The politics of the situation may even have been influenced by the fact that Annie was nearly five foot six inches (170 cm) to Harry's five foot three and half (163 cm). However, offensive threats and boasts alone cannot be regarded as a sign of guilt.

Eugenia was guilty of lying, perhaps of fantasising, and of extreme manipulativeness. Although her existence as a man presupposed lies, and her survival depended on her ability to emotionally manipulate the people around her, much of her lying was unnecessary for the support of her male identity. That Harry Crawford tried to isolate Annie Birkett from her sister, and to maintain himself in good stead with neighbours and friends by giving them versions of events most favourable to himself is fairly evident. To be capable of violence is another matter.

Josephine's statement to police provides an indication that Eugenia had made an attempt to smother her as a baby, or at least threatened to (a threat which Mariana De Angelis had an interest in repeating to Josephine to ensure her own place in the little girl's affections). This can also be put in a different context. Dr Anne Summers, in *Damned Whores and God's Police*, comments that infanticide, as well as abortion, was widespread in Australia at the turn of the century.[9]

Although the fundamental unit of society was

---

9   Page 320, Pelican edition, 1975.

Eugenia: A Man

the family, and although the prevailing philosophy was that producing 'sons' for Australia was a good idea, economic conditions—as well as the hazards to women's health presented by repeated childbearing—often made these large families undesirable. A decline in the birth rate between 1886 and 1901 (with no significant decline in the marriage rate) indicates that women were taking control of their own fertility, sometimes by dubious means.

Contraceptive devices and abortifacients were available in chemist shops and were widely, if euphemistically, advertised in newspapers and magazines. These included condoms, pills, pessaries and douches, often described as being designed to prevent 'irregularities'. Advertisements for 'lying-in' homes also appeared, masking the services of abortionists.

Summers points out that it was still not legally proscribed to kill a child in the process of birth. Death certificates were not required for newborn babies, nor did they have to be buried in a cemetery. Deaths of older children were sometimes classified in the same way. The deaths of as many as 15,000 babies were attributed to overdoses of pacifying patent medicines in one year. It is reasonable to conclude, she argues, that not all these deaths were accidental.

Between 1891 and 1900 one quarter of all first births were illegitimate, while a further quarter were born within nine months of marriage, Summers continues. The births of Annie Birkett herself, Harry Bell Birkett, Josephine and Josephine's own baby all fit into this pattern, unless the first was premature. The prevailing belief that single women in the early part of the last century were not sexually active seems to be a middle-class myth invented in the post World War II period.

In this context, Eugenia's alleged attempt to smother her baby, while completely abhorrent, was probably not especially unusual. She may have known of women who had done precisely this. The important thing is that, although the pregnancy must have been repugnant to her, she did not—or did not succeed in—taking any such measures herself.

However, there is reasonable evidence to suggest that she went further in her attempts to get rid of the boy Harry Birkett, although both times in the final instant she drew back. Again, a spoken threat to kill someone is hardly a sign of guilt. If Harry Crawford did say to Mrs Schieblich that he was going to kill the boy before setting out for Bellevue Hill (an area Eugenia would have been familiar with from her days at Double Bay), it may have been from a desire that someone should stop him.

In the end, only Annie Birkett died, and whether Eugenia knowingly intended to kill her remains uncertain at best.

During Eugenia's trial the question was never finally answered as to whether Harry Crawford had allegedly committed a premeditated murder, a crime of passion, or an uncontrolled drunken act. There was no direct evidence to suggest that Harry had lured Annie into the wilderness with the intention of killing her. One or both were drinking whisky at the time. Harry, drunk and in the midst of a violent argument, may have struck Annie unintentionally hard, and then in panic and remorse set fire to her unconscious body, thinking she was dead. What was the weapon? He may have struck her with his fist, causing her to fall on the nearby rock. Was there provocation? No explanation of the exact circumstances of the killing seems to have been offered by defence or prosecution.

And if he did strike her without the intent of killing her, and then set fire to the body in panic, was he guilty of premeditated murder, as the prosecution tried to suggest?

Twenty-Nine

ON 19 FEBRUARY 1931, as the spans of the-soon-to-be-completed Sydney Harbour Bridge drew slowly together and the city struggled in the grip of the Great Depression, Eugenia left Long Bay to discover a city where unemployed workers marched in the streets and camped in tent cities in the Domain, and where motor cars were five times more numerous than eleven years before. For three years, moving from place to place and taking whatever employment she could get, Eugenia was swallowed up by the city.

The second last time that Dr Moran saw Eugenia Falleni was in 1934, when she walked into his medical chambers at 185 Macquarie Street, dressed as a woman, behind an Italian woman with incurable breast cancer. Possibly she had come to translate for her. Moran had visited Eugenia in prison twice, so perhaps there was a degree of trust between the doctor and the ex-prisoner.

Eugenia, appearing aged and grey, signalled behind the Italian woman's back that Moran should disclose nothing. She still walked, he noted, with the stride of a man.

After the examination, Eugenia came back into the room on the pretence of asking a further question.

Eugenia: A Man

She confided in a whisper that she was now a 'useful help' in this couple's household—although they were obviously not well off, Moran had observed. Eugenia believed that they knew nothing about her past.

A few weeks later she came to see him again, this time to ask his help in getting an invalid pension. Moran gave her the necessary certificate, but the application was refused.

It appeared, Moran found out later, that the Italian couple knew Eugenia's story well, but out of kindness they feigned ignorance. They had taken her in, he wrote, out of a sense of charity that the Australian government, having released her after eleven years for exemplary conduct, did not share.

Soon after this Eugenia followed the example of her landladies Bombelli and Schieblich, and set herself up in a small business of her own. Calling herself Jean Ford, she rented out inexpensive rooms in a leased Victorian terrace house at 27 Glenmore Road, Paddington, a mile or two from her starting point at Double Bay.

Newspaper stories in the *Sun* and *Sun-Herald* in 1958 and 1961 both maintained that Mrs Jean Ford was respected and admired as an honest and decent woman by her lodgers, although a writer in the *Sun* of 14 August 1952 found her 'sombre and reticent'. Four years later she sold the goodwill in the business to an agent for £100.

At 63, with grey hair and stooped shoulders, she had collected the money in cash and was carrying it in her handbag when, on 9 June 1938, apparently distracted, she stepped out from the kerb on Oxford Street near Hopetoun Avenue, Paddington, and under the wheels of a car driven by William Lamb, a carpenter from Bexley.

Perhaps at that moment her head was full of plans for what she would do next. She had paid her debt, was free at last of the disgrace that had prevented her return to her family so many years before. Perhaps it is not unreasonable to conjecture that she might have dreamed of going home.

Eugenia died next day at Sydney Hospital in Macquarie Street of injuries to the chest and brain, and was buried at the Church of England cemetery at Rookwood the day after that. A fingerprint check by the police had revealed her real identity.

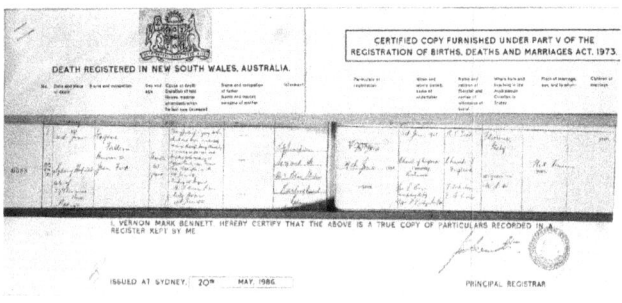

Death certificate, 'Eugene Falleni known as Gene Ford', dated 10 June 1938. Photo: NSW Registry of Births, Deaths and Marriages.

Sergeant L. G. Simpson of No. 3 Police Station, Darlinghurst, supplied details for the death certificate. He stated in a report to the coroner that he had information that Falleni had an illegitimate daughter who had died in the Women's Hospital, Crown Street, and that the daughter had a child who was now in a convent at Narellan.

No one came forward to claim the body.

A newspaper account in the *Sunday Sun* and *Guardian* of 12 June 1938 maintained that, 'to the day of her death, Eugene Falleni professed her innocence. She believed, as a result of her release, that the Crown had learned facts which proved her innocence'. The story continued, 'She was well-educated, a good conversationalist, and made every effort to live down her past.'

The *Daily Telegraph* of 13 June 1938 quoted a man who had been her business confidant for four years, and who was apparently astounded to learn her identity:

> She came to me whenever she conducted any business. She could neither read nor write, and she used to sign her documents with a mark. She told me about bits of her past life, but she never mentioned the 'man-woman' matter. In business dealings she was scrupulously honest.

'She was tall, thin and very active, and weighed about six stone, seven pounds,' he added, somewhat mysteriously.

On 13 June 1938 a Wellington newspaper reported Eugenia's death in Sydney three days before. On 15 June, her father Luigi Falleni, aged 86, died at 23 Wilson Street, Wellington. Her mother Isola Falleni would die in hospital on 3 July, two weeks later. Both Isola and Luigi were buried at Karori.

H. M. Moran himself died at sixty on 20 November 1945, in Cambridge in England, not long after completing his third book, *In My Fashion*, an autobiographical work detailing his experiences as a doctor in Europe during World War II. One of his achievements outside the medical field was to be instrumental in initiating the teaching of Italian at the University of Sydney.

Thirty

THERE WERE no Fallenis in the Sydney telephone book when I looked in 1986. Harry Birkett, in his eighties, might have still been alive, but I did not try to track him down, nor his descendants. Nor did I try to find Josephine's daughter, although I imagined her growing up, unknowing and perhaps with a different name, within the still walls of a convent much like the one I had visited when I first discovered, by accident, Eugenia's existence. It seemed a coincidence that a story that had begun for me in a convent should end in one.

Eugenia did not make the transition from one gender to another without becoming a casualty, and taking other casualties with her. There appeared to be no conclusions to be drawn from any of it, except that if Harry Crawford had lived in a different time and place, perhaps the death of Annie Birkett might not have occurred as it had.

One of the last things that I did, as the winter of 1986 approached, was to go out to Rookwood cemetery. Eugenia was buried in the Anglican section, according to her death certificate. The cemetery stretched for miles. Each ethnic community—Chinese, clustered around a small red temple; Jewish, with green, neatly clipped lawns and black, monolithic memorial stones; Greek Orthodox and Russian Orthodox with their ornate crosses; Muslim, and Hindu—had its own city of stones separated by bleak expanses of wintry grass. Somewhere among them, nearly half a century before, the Reverend R. O. Todd and two witnesses, T. Whelan and E. H. Wade, had stood with one Leo Brian, undertaker, employed by a Mr P. Kirby and Son, and seen Eugenia buried.

The man behind the desk at the Anglican office looked at me curiously, and then went into a back room and pulled down some old ledgers. He was away quite a long time. When he came back he wrote a couple of numbers on a small card. Eugenia was buried in plot no. 3223, he said, but the grave was unmarked. I should look for 'Gough' and 'Morris', Nos. 3221 and 3226, and in a three-foot stretch of ground about halfway between them, I should find where Eugenia lay.

When I asked why an Italian woman, who would have been at least nominally Catholic, would have been buried in the Anglican section, he told me that the undertaker would have bought the cheapest lot he could, regardless of her faith. It would have been a contract funeral, supplied at the public expense. It was ironic, I thought, that even in death Eugenia was out of place. I doubted that she would have cared.

I found the section with some difficulty in an overgrown and neglected corner of the cemetery, near some dying poplar trees. It was covered in dead grass. A dark-haired Italian man, monosyllabic and perhaps a little apprehensive at being approached, showed me where to look for the numbers, barely legible, on the older sandstone graves. There was no one else to ask. Then he went back to mowing the grass strips between some distant rows. It was a cold, grey day and the wind was icy; the sound of the noisy mower jarred like a toothache.

I wandered up and down the uneven rows until I found the patch of ground that must have been Eugenia's. None of the nearby graves was recent, none had fresh flowers. The only touch of colour was some plastic roses in a capsized glass jar a little distance away. I had not thought to bring any flowers, but there was a wattle tree at the end of the row, and I picked her a small bunch from that. I left the pungent yellow blossoms among the dead grass.

A Postscript

EUGENIA: A MAN was published in late May 1988 in a small flurry of publicity. One Tuesday morning soon afterwards, while I was being interviewed by George Negus on the 'Today' program on Channel 9, a woman called Nancy Cracknell telephoned the station from Lakemba and asked to speak to me.

Tuesday was the day the pest control people were coming to fumigate the house, so she was having an early breakfast, Nancy told me when I rang her back. She had switched the television to one of the morning chat shows—she enjoyed those programs because it was like meeting new people, she said. The pretty girl announcer whose name she couldn't remember had been saying something about transsexuals, but she wasn't really listening because it wasn't something that interested her. Then she heard the name mentioned, Eugenia Falleni.

'That's Arthur Whitby's mother-in-law!' she thought.

Mrs Cracknell was aged 72 when we talked. Arthur Whitby had been her mother's husband for sixteen years. Before that, Whitby had been married to Eugenia's daughter Josephine Falleni. I felt slightly at a loss: I had never considered Eugenia as a mother-in-law.

Eugenia: A Man

Nancy's mother Alice was 'not a tart' (as Nancy put it), but Nancy herself and her brother and half brother were all illegitimate, she continued. Her mother had come from a family of eleven children in Junee: or rather, it was more like three families because, although they all had the same father, there were long gaps between the children—and so during the Great War, Alice and one of her sisters were sent to Sydney to work. They found a verandah room above the main road at Darlington. Both were young and inexperienced, so Nancy—née Azile Elizabeth Nichols—was born in 1916 as a result of an encounter with an unknown man, a 'ship in the night'. Work was hard in those days, and there was no money; what else was there for young girls to do but 'make love down the paddock'? Eventually her grandmother came to Sydney to look after the two sisters, and all three women lived together.

Nancy remembered growing up with no shoes and on the dole, but she was determined to better herself. She wanted love, and eventually she found it with a man who loved her: a good man, Stan Cracknell, a linotype operator who worked for the *Mirror* and for the government, she told me. A Union man. He had died some sixteen years ago, and there were a hundred cards at his funeral.

Arthur Whitby, who was to become her stepfather, was a sailor: a dark, Celtic-looking man. He'd been on HMS *Sydney* during the sinking of the German raider *Emden*. Moody, he could be violent-tempered, according to Nancy. He'd met Eugenia's daughter Josephine—Josie—when they were both very young. He'd got Josie Falleni into trouble, Nancy thought, and had had to marry her. Their daughter Rita was born around 1920, when Arthur was about 23 and Josie 21.

Arthur Whitby had married three women in all: her mother Alice Nicholls was the second. After Alice had died in 1939, when Nancy was 23, he'd married the last one. When this woman died too, her children had tried to get her furniture back from him, and he barricaded himself inside the house; but when Nancy went to see him, his place was so decrepit that she couldn't see what they'd made the fuss about. Arthur was a quiet, sulky man. He hit Nancy only once—and then she'd left home, at eighteen. But afterwards she'd patched things up with him, and he came to her wedding.

Josie and Arthur had lived together at 54 Darlington Road off Cleveland Street in Newtown. Nancy believed Eugenia had sometimes lived there too. This must have been in 1919 or early 1920—Nancy herself was then aged about four. At this time 'Gene' Falleni was dressed as a woman. Nancy remembered her as a 'black blob' sitting on the gas box. As a small child, she felt that Gene had an aura about her that made her afraid.

Josie had died soon after this, of tuberculosis, Nancy believed; she had heard that it was a result of being kicked in the breast by a horse, but how could that cause TB? Josie had died very young, however: her daughter Rita was only about three years old. Arthur had a sister who lived at Stanmore, and at some point Nancy remembered seeing Rita there with her—a small child with a mass of dark curls. Then Rita was put into a convent at Narellan.

After Josie died, Arthur had gone to live in a boarding house near their room: that was how he courted her mother Alice—she would be leaning over the balcony and he would call up to her on his way home. Alice had been in her thirties when she met Arthur, but she pretended to be much younger, of course. Arthur was then about 26. Nancy was a bit vague about the exact dates. But Nancy was four years older than Rita, and Arthur had married Alice when Nancy was aged about eight, so this must have been about 1924. Nancy by this time was going to school in Darlington, and she lived with her mother and Arthur for ten years, until she left home in 1934.

Alice had wanted to bring Rita home from the convent after they were married, but Arthur wanted to leave her there—better to 'let sleeping dogs lie', he said. He had hinted that she might not be his child after all. But then, in 1936, when Rita turned sixteen and came out of the convent, Alice worried that, through Rita, Gene Falleni might find Arthur. Gene had threatened to kill him. She had already stabbed him with a knife, after an argument. She was a bad woman, Nancy thought.

But why would Gene attack Arthur? I asked.

For making Josie pregnant, Nancy believed. Or—here Nancy laughed—maybe he'd 'slung it up at her'? At any rate, both her mother and Arthur were on tenterhooks for a while.

When Nancy met Rita again, Rita resented her—and with good reason, thought Nancy, as she had lived at home with Arthur, Rita's father, while Rita was kept in the convent. Then Rita went off to live at Kings Cross. Although Kings Cross was a different place in those days, Nancy felt Rita might be on the way down. She was very pretty.

Josie herself had been born after 'a sailor forced his way into the bathroom' on the ship, Nancy believed. Something like that.

We chatted for some three quarters of an hour. Nancy had a cousin who knew Rita, she told me, who lived in Paddington now and had a different name through marriage. She thought she might ring her. A week or so later we had a second conversation. Nancy had talked to her cousin, and this relative thought that Rita knew nothing of Eugenia's story, and 'it would kill her if she found out'. So—once again—we decided to let sleeping dogs lie. I would not try to contact Rita for further information, I promised. Some good had come of it, however, Nancy ended, as she'd had a 'good old talk' with her cousin whom she hadn't seen for years.

What impressed me about Nancy Cracknell was her open-mindedness and lack of prudery about the circumstances of her own birth and her mother's life as a battler. She seemed very non-judgmental, apart from her instinctive childish dislike of Eugenia. Like Olga Falleni in New Zealand, her common sense and good humour made her a delight to talk to.

NEVERTHELESS, when I looked over my notes and started working out some exact dates, I was again rather startled. If what Nancy told me was essentially correct, what hadn't emerged at the trial was that while Eugenia, as Harry Crawford, was living as husband and wife with Lizzy Allison in the year or so before his arrest, he was also still keeping up a simultaneous identity—as 'Gene Falleni', and dressing as a woman—and had spent some time at least with Josephine and Arthur in Darlington Road.

Josephine, it emerged, had married Arthur Raymond Whitby, age 24, a sailor, at an Anglican church at St Peters on 18 August 1920, the day before her mother was committed for trial. Josephine was now 21. If it was a pregnancy that had prompted the wedding, it did not come to fruition. Their daughter Rita Josephine Whitby was not born until 20 November 1921, fifteen months later, while Eugenia was in Long Bay.

Josephine had died of pulmonary tuberculosis at 17 Crown Street, East Sydney—perhaps some sort of private nursing home—on 19 December 1924, aged 26. The informant was A. R. Whitby, of 54 Darlington Road, and her mother's name was given as Eugenie Falleni. John Jamieson—the city coroner who had ordered Annie Birkett's exhumation—dispensed with an inquest. Josie Whitby left Mortuary Station in Regent Street for the Catholic section of the Rookwood Cemetery the following day.

Even allowing for some inexactness with dates on Nancy's part, it appeared that Whitby had formed an attachment with Nancy's mother, Alice Maud Nichols, immediately upon Josie's death, if not before—a union that would last until Alice's own death in late 1939. While Josie was ill, three-year-old Rita had been cared for initially by Arthur's sister at Stanmore, before being placed with the Sisters of the Good Samaritan at the Mater Dei Orphanage at Narellan, also known as 'Wivenhoe'. And if Nancy, at the age of eight or nine, believed that her mother and stepfather had wed in

1924, when the couple had started living together, she was mistaken. According to the NSW Registry, the marriage of Alice and Arthur—who by this date had left the Royal Australian Navy to become a telephone linesman or postal worker—did not take place until 5 January 1934, the year that Nancy left home.

In the meantime—to Arthur's evident consternation—Eugenia was released from gaol in 1931, when Rita was aged about eleven. Would she come looking for Arthur, and seek retribution for his treatment of Rita, her granddaughter—or even of Josephine herself?

However, from Nancy's account, Eugenia appeared to have made no attempt to find Rita, and Rita herself apparently lived in ignorance of her grandmother's notoriety. On 19 October 1950, Rita Whitby, machinist, aged 29, married Thomas Elvy, a motor driver, 27, at St Michael's Anglican church in Sydney. Sleeping dogs had indeed been allowed to lie, according to Nancy—at least for the moment.

SOME TIME after this the telephone rang again and a man asked to speak to me: it was one of those calls where you know that the caller has checked the directory but isn't entirely sure whether the number found is the one that is wanted.

'I rang to congratulate you on the book—' said the voice.

'Thank you,' I said. 'To whom am I speaking?'

'Stewart Robson.'

Again I was momentarily at a loss. The name was familiar, although I couldn't immediately place it. Suddenly it dawned on me: I was being telephoned by one of the characters in my book. Stewart Robson was the detective sergeant who had arrested Eugenia Falleni and conducted the investigation that led to her conviction.

'I am the grandson,' he explained.

'And are you a policeman too?'

'No, I'm a private detective.'

I laughed.

Stewart Robson had three things to reveal:

He had hero-worshipped his grandfather.

He had some of his grandfather's files.

He thought we should meet.

The next thing he asked me was what star sign I was. When I said 'Pisces', he said he'd thought so. A lot of detectives were Pisces, he told me.

I was a bit suspicious about this. I wished I'd said nothing; asked him why first. It sounded like one of those lines designed to flatter and gain your confidence—or to extract information.

'I wouldn't have thought an analytical mind would take much notice of astrology,' I said.

We had a bit of further chat: did I know that Lillian Armfield, Australia's first policewoman, had questioned Eugene Falleni with Robson's grandfather when she was arrested? She had written about it in a book, he told me.

I was about to go overseas for several weeks, I told Robson eventually. He should call me when I got back. Then I hung up.

I never heard from him again.

I still wonder sometimes about those files.

LILLIAN MAY ARMFIELD had been in her

mid-thirties and a special constable for five years when she came in contact with Eugenia Falleni, I discovered. Her recollections of the case, as apparently told to well-known crime journalist Vince Kelly in his book *Rugged Angel*[10] in 1961, were wrong in many details. But then, at that date the events were forty years in the past and Armfield herself was 77 years old. I suspected that Kelly had filled out his account from some of the more notoriously unreliable newspaper reports, especially in regard to occurrences that Armfield had not personally witnessed. He had called the chapter 'Cabin-Boy Mother'.

Nevertheless, it seemed that Armfield was at the Central Police Station on other business when Detective Sergeant Robson and Detective Constable Watkins brought in Harry Crawford for questioning on Monday 5 July 1920.

Crawford was 'small, active and alert' and 'looking wildly about like a trapped thing', according to Armfield. After asking if he was to be locked up, and then requesting to go to the women's ward if he were, Crawford had 'glared' at them when they laughed at what they thought was his impudent joke. 'Falleni was sullen, and her small dark eyes were savage,' Armfield went on.

At face value, this suggests that, rather than taunting her with their prior knowledge, Robson and his fellow officers were indeed unaware at that point of Falleni's true sex. Given that they had already extensively questioned Harry Birkett and his aunt, who both knew, this seemed unlikely. Armfield also evidently witnessed Eugenia's examination by the Government

---

10   Vince Kelly, *Rugged Angel: The Amazing Career of Policewoman Lillian Armfield*, Angus & Robertson, Sydney, 1961.

Medical officer: 'She appeared so mortified at having her sex exposed that the murder she was charged with was almost unimportant compared with it.'

This view was shared by Robson and Watkins, according to Vince Kelly: 'In every conversation they had with Falleni, she spoke as if she were a man, with a man's viewpoint, and in the soft, husky, deep voice that was more masculine than feminine.'

'After we had unmasked her deception, she got into a panic again when we told her we were intending to take her to her home address in Durham Street, Stanmore,' continued Lillian Armfield. 'I couldn't understand why, until she seized my hand and said, "I don't want my wife to know anything about this…".'

A large part of a female special constable's duties was to ensure the safety and welfare of women and girls while they were in male police custody, and so probably it was in this role that Armfield accompanied her fellow officers to the house in Durham Street.

According to Armfield, Lizzie Allison was not at home when they arrived, and Falleni seemed relieved, but soon became agitated again when Robson questioned her about the locked suitcase in the bedroom. According to the trial evidence, however, Allison was present, and constantly weeping, during the search—but perhaps not in the room when Falleni begged the officers (referring to the artificial phallus, or 'successful means of her deception'), 'Take it away with you! Don't let her see it! Don't let her know what's in it!'

Later that afternoon, after Eugenia had been charged at the Police Court in Liverpool Street, Lizzie Allison came to the Central Police station and demanded to see her husband, Harry Crawford. By her own account, it fell to Armfield to tell Lizzie, as gently as she could, that she could not be the wife of the person they had in custody. Lizzie Allison stared at her incredulously, and asked, 'You mean he's a bigamist?'

When Armfield explained that Crawford had been found to be a woman, Lizzie Allison flatly refused to believe it. In a state of shock, she again asked if she could see her husband, but the prisoner refused to see her.

Lizzie Allison held out in her denial until Robson opened the suitcase and showed her the object they had found in it: a detail also confirmed by H. M. Moran. Then, according to Armfield, she left the station without a word.

Soon after this she changed her address and could not be located again.

AMONG OTHER communications in the intervening years, in the early 1990s a plump package arrived in the mail from a Mr J. A. Knight of Bondi Junction, enclosing a bundle of newspaper cuttings. Mr Knight had been investigating Eugenia's case himself, he wrote in his covering letter, and had recently come upon my book.

Mr Knight had a rather alarming theory, it emerged. Not only had Eugenia Falleni killed a man in New Zealand, he believed, and possibly Mariana De Angelis in Double Bay as well, but also a black woman who worked in the same laundry in New South Head Road, whose disappearance the police had been unable account for. His reasoning was that Eugenia's eyes—according to the prison record card—were blue, and many notorious murderers had blue eyes. (Mr Knight wrote again later to apologise if my own eyes were blue.)

More importantly, among Mr Knight's newspaper clippings (which included several about his own arrest for making menacing phone calls to a judge) was an extract from a New Zealand Births, Deaths and Marriages Registry. This indicated, again rather startlingly, that before reaching Australia Eugenia married a man whose name was transcribed as 'Brateli Innoconte'.

An application to the same Registry produced a handwritten record revealing that on 14 September 1894, at the Wellington Registrar's office, nineteen-year-old Eugenia—here given as 'Ugenia'—had in fact wed Braseli Innocenti (or possibly 'Innocente'), aged 31, son of Angiolo Innocenti, a farmer, and his wife Maria, née Giacopassi. Eugenia's father Luigi and another man, Caesari Pierotti, had witnessed the marriage, and Eugenia had signed her name with a cross, annotated 'her mark'.

Braseli Innocenti, born in Italy, resident in Wellington, was described as an 'Image maker': probably a *figurinaio*, or maker of plaster figurines. Many such image makers—*figurinai di Gesso*, or *figuristi*—mainly from the Tuscan province of Lucca, had emigrated to the New World in the 19th century, including to New Zealand and Australia.

Caesari Pierroti, now known as 'Cesar' or Charles, and now a fishmonger of Tory Street, seemed an odd choice for a second witness. Like Eugenia's father he had once been a coachman and a fisherman, but unlike the respectable Luigi Falleni he cropped up frequently in Wellington court reports, brought before the magistrate for drunkenness, violence and bad language; once for fighting a duel, at other times for assaulting his wife Luisa, or allowing his horses to stray, or catching undersized fish, in which cases he often represented himself. He himself was also litigious, frequently quarrelling with other men and bringing minor charges against them. In the small Italian community in Wellington, was he a friend of the bridegroom? Or was he some old associate of Luigi's who would have no scruples about helping him to force his troublesome daughter into an unwelcome marriage, ostensibly for her own good?

The union was not a success. Ten months on, items appeared in a number of New Zealand newspapers disclosing that Eugenia—who was not named—had run away from her husband on discovering that her marriage was bigamous.[11] Under such generally admiring headlines as 'A WOMAN IN BOY'S CLOTHES', 'ROMANCE IN REAL LIFE: A GIRL'S COURAGE' and 'A PLUCKY GIRL', these reported that Eugenia had turned up in Wellington again, seeking work in a ceramics factory or a brickyard before taking refuge with the Salvation Army.

> STRANGE STORY, Wellington July 22:
> Among women at the Salvation Army's Pauline Home is one, who, being unhappy in her own family, married about nine months ago, and removed to Auckland, where she found that her supposed husband was a married

---

11   My thanks to Mark Tedeschi for alerting me to this last development.

man with a family. She left him at once and returned to Wellington, where she donned boy's clothes, and obtained work in a drain-pipe factory. She was recognised after working for a week, and accepted the shelter offered by the Salvationists. The girl is only 21 years old.

> —*The Colonist*, 23 July 1895, page 3:
> TELEGRAMS

A year later again, similar newspaper paragraphs recorded that Eugenia—now calling herself 'Lena Salette'—had been arrested for vagrancy in Masterton, a town about fifty miles away. Masterton's local paper, the *Feilding Star* of 28 July 1896, revealed that 'Lena' had tried to find work there as a domestic servant. Failing this, she had put on men's clothing and applied to the Benevolent Society for a job, but the Society's Secretary, a Mr T. Duncan, had rather uncharitably called the police. Charged with having no means of support, Eugenia pleaded guilty, maintaining that someone had 'put her up to' the impersonation. Sobbing, she told the magistrate she was willing to return to her friends in Wellington, and if 'let off' would never do it again, whereupon she was discharged.

'Her hair was cut short and her voice resembled that of a boy of seventeen,' reported another paper, which recorded that she was dressed as a stable boy. 'She also smoked a cigarette.'

The *Wairarapa Star* added that she was 'of rather becoming appearance'.[12]

---

12   See also *North Otago Times*, 6 August 1896, p. 4; *Poverty Bay Herald*, 6 August 1896, p. 4.

THE IDENTITY of the sailor 'Martello', Josephine's alleged father, still niggled at the back of my mind. Even with the wealth of newspapers and shipping lists now easily searchable on the internet, no likely candidate had appeared in the period after July 1896, when Eugenia had faced the court at Masterton, and 19 September 1898, when she gave birth to her baby at Double Bay in Sydney. By these calculations, however, Eugenia must have become pregnant in December 1897.

Then, one day as I randomly Googled the name 'Captain Martello', one showed up as the master of a tramp steamer called the *Flamenco*, sunk by the German raider *Möwe* some 310 miles off Pernambuco on 6 February 1916 while en route from Newport in Wales to Valparaiso in Chile, hauling a cargo of coal. With the loss of one life, it seemed the captain and the rest of the crew had been saved.

A little more searching established that this 'Captain Martello' was in fact a misprint for a Captain Norman Martorell, who in September 1896 was listed as the Second Mate on the *Orotava*, an Orient & Pacific Steam Navigation Co. vessel working the London to Sydney mail route via Auckland and Wellington. Martorell, of Spanish descent but born in Liverpool around 1867, had gone to sea in the days of sail as an apprentice at fourteen. By 1897, risen through the ranks and sailing on the *Orotava* with an English crew, he was nearly thirty. The ship's route from the UK via the Suez and Colombo took in Fremantle, Adelaide, Melbourne, Hobart and Sydney before New Zealand, so if Eugenia were on board, she may have made a round trip to Britain before being put ashore again in Australia.

Had second mate Norman Martorell merely befriended Eugenia, and inspired her to use his name? Or was he indeed Josie's father? After World War I Martorell continued his successful career as a ship's captain before eventually emigrating to Canada, where in 1933 he was appointed Port Warden at Churchill, near Montreal, and died in 1950.

JOSEPHINE'S daughter Rita was also never really to know her father. After her mother's death in 1924 she had little further contact with Arthur Whitby for 50 years. In 1944, some five years after the death of his second wife Alice, Whitby had married a third time, to a Dorothy Frances MacCarthy.

When Dorothy died in 1974, I would learn, Arthur finally contacted Rita, and she and her husband Thomas Elvy, with their two children, had visited him in Campbelltown.[13] Arthur Whitby died at Bellingen on 16 October 1986, keeping many of his secrets: according to my informant Nancy Cracknell, Rita knew nothing about her grandmother Eugenia even in 1988. Rita would die in 1995, at 74. Nancy Cracknell, née Nichols—happily married Stanley Herbert Cracknell from 1940—died in August 1997.

As for Mr J. A. Knight, who had first put me on the trail of Eugenia's marriage in New Zealand, I later discovered he had put his considerable talent for genealogical research in public libraries to the task of creating 31 separate identities, which had enabled him, over several years, to fraudulently claim Centrelink payments totalling some $474,000. In 2003 he was sentenced to eight years jail. I could only salute his ingenuity.

13　　Mark Tedeschi, *Eugenia*, Simon and Schuster, Sydney 2012, p. 237.

SEVERAL PEOPLE alerted me to the odd resonances of Eugenia's story with the iconography of Saint Eugenia, whose name—uncommon in Italy, but meaning also of good or noble birth—had been passed down to Eugenia Falleni from her maternal grandmother. Said to have been the daughter of an Alexandrian noble who governed Egypt, the earlier Eugenia, with her servants Protus and Hyacinth, had left her father's house dressed in men's clothing and was baptized a Christian by Helenus, bishop of Heliopolis. While still disguised as a man she became an Abbot and—in a story thought to be apocryphal—cured a woman of serious illness. The lady, enamoured of her benefactor, made advances and, on being rebuffed, publicly accused the Abbot of adultery. Eugenia was brought before a court where, still in male disguise, she faced her father as her judge. Forced to reveal her female identity, she was exonerated. When her father Philip, who had also converted to Christianity and become Bishop of Alexandria, was executed, Eugenia and her household moved to Rome. Here she brought many to the Christian faith, especially young women, but was beheaded on 25 December 258, in the reign of the Emperor Valerian, along with Protus and Hyacinth.

Eugenia's unmarked grave at Rookwood Cemetery in 2010. The head of the grave is approximately at centre, marked by a small bunch of flowers. Photo: Author, private collection.

Acknowledgements

IN THE MID-1980s when I first started investigating the story of Eugenia Falleni, little was certain—not even Eugenia's true birth name—and nothing was easy to find out. Searchable online catalogues and archival resources barely existed outside universities. Armed with a few small clues, one visited public libraries and thumbed though hard copies of newspapers at around the right month and year, hoping that a headline, a name, a news story might catch the eye. At the NSW State Archives, piles of handwritten ledgers were brought out—books of evidence, case notes, trials transcripts—again to be physically leafed through, on the off-chance the relevant court records might have survived.

For assistance in the research of the first edition of this book I thank the State Library of New South Wales (and particularly the staff of the Newspaper Room), the Mitchell Library, the New South Wales Government Archives and their photographic service, the Solicitor for Public Prosecutions, the Police Community Relations Bureau, the late Mr John Partridge of the Department of Corrective Services, the Australian Institute of Criminology, Woollahra Library, James

Holledge, Hank Van Zuilekon, Alan Sharpe, Dr T. G. H. Oettle, Dr Neil Buhrich, Tristan Fonlladosa, Kay Carston and Andrew Cutler, Ros Nelson, and Mary Falloon. In New Zealand the National Library of Wellington, the National Archives of New Zealand, and the Maritime Museum of Wellington were helpful. My gratitude is due also to the late Rosemary Creswell. Most of all, I would like to thank the Falleni family, who met my inquisitiveness with grace and kindness.

After the book was published my correspondence with Githa Falleni continued amicably for several years, with regular Christmas cards arriving. I never learned from Githa, as I did later from one of her daughters, that there had been 'a terrible row' between Githa and their 'Nana', who had disowned their branch of the family for speaking to me. Githa died in July 2010. I am grateful for her generosity of spirit.

Since *Eugenia: A Man* was published, Eugenia Falleni has become the subject of a musical, a play, several short films and a television feature, and her image has featured in various art exhibitions and photographic and museum displays. A number of academic papers have examined her case, and several feature film scripts have been attempted and bitten the dust. Most of these have acknowledged *Eugenia: A Man* as their starting point or primary resource. More recently, NSW Public Prosecutor Mark Tedeschi has written a speculative biography, re-arguing Eugenia's case and expertly examining the legal processes around her trial. I thank him for his generosity in sharing information that has emerged since the first publication of my book. Mark Tedeschi's conclusion resembles mine: Eugenia should never have been found guilty of murder on the evidence offered at the trial.

In the interim, too, the discourse on gender dysphoria has moved on. In the 1980s I moved loosely between the categories 'cross dresser' and 'transsexual' in my description. Since the book was first published, there has been lively, even contentious, discussion as to where to place Eugenia along the transgender spectrum, sometimes framing her story in theory that did not exist at the time of my original research. What Eugenia might have thought about this, nobody knows.

My aim, then as now, was not to speak for Eugenia, but to try to establish the verifiable facts where possible. Thus, apart from some minor clarifications and corrections, in this new edition I have preferred to leave the main text largely as an artefact of its time.

In 2014 I owe a further debt of gratitude to the late Nancy Cracknell, John Adrian Knight, Barbara Mobbs, Bruce Robertson and Ray Sinclair Wood. Thanks also to Rod Morrison, Jon MacDonald and all at Xoum.

www.ingramcontent.com/pod-product-compliance
Lightning Source LLC
Chambersburg PA
CBHW031423150426
43191CB00006B/373